# What others are saying about *Best Year Ever!*

*It was a pleasure to serve as State Superintendent of Schools the year Bill Cecil was chosen to represent the fantastic Michigan teachers as "Teacher of the Year!" Bill has a contagious, "can do attitude" that helps propel students and adults forward to accomplish the task at hand. Perhaps the highest praise I can give to Bill is that I only wish my children could have had him as their teacher! Michigan is blessed to have many great teachers, and Bill is at the top of the class.*

**— Tom Watkins, President and CEO TDW, Associates**
**Michigan Superintendent of Schools 2001-2005**

*Bill Cecil's book* **Best Year Ever! Winning Strategies to Thrive In Today's Classroom** *is a life-saver for new teachers. It includes many tips and strategies that REALLY work! Last year, as a new teacher, I continuously struggled with classroom management. As I integrated Bill's strategies into my own teaching, I watched my children thrive off their own personal successes and the successes of their peers. They developed pride and responsibility for themselves and this in turn created a learning community with minimum behavioral disruptions. With the success and integration of the* **Best Year Ever!** *strategies into my own classroom, my management program NOW works for me. Teaching has become a rewarding career choice, and I am grateful to be part of this wonderful profession.*

**—Jennifer Sovey, 1st Grade Teacher**
**Zela Davis Elementary School, Hawthorne, California**

*The 21st Century new teacher needs as many tools in their box as they can acquire. Bill Cecil has presented at our Future and New Teachers Conference twice in the last three years. His message, his passion for teaching, and his practical teaching tips are echoed often by our new preservice teachers. Without a doubt, he has tried and true information and it is refreshing, as an educator, to hear preservice teachers use his ideas and suggestions. More important, Bill's ideas are effective.*

**— Mary C. Belknap**
**Teacher Education Coordinator/Professor Jackson Community College;**
**National Association of Community Colleges in Teacher Education Preparation**

*Using* **Best Year Ever!** *for three years has taught me the essential ingredients for building a winning classroom community. As a teacher, not only am I responsible for delivering the curriculum, I also reinforce teamwork, cooperation, goal setting, accountability, and a sense of being the best person you can be, as well as doing my best to enjoy each and every day. Aren't these the real skills needed to have a positive, productive, and successful life?*

**— Denise Kehren, 6th Grade Teacher**
**Waverly East Intermediate School, Lansing, Michigan**

*I have first-hand knowledge of the strategies Bill Cecil provided to our K-12 teaching staff. His in-service was by far the best we've ever had in my twelve years as superintendent. Our beginning teachers to our veteran teachers are using his team building strategies in their classrooms. Bill has explained how the positive classroom environment can lead to more rigor, relevance, and relationships that are needed in today's education world.*

**— Denny Chartier, Superintendent,
Iron Mountain Public Schools**

*I have had the privilege of attending Bill Cecil's* **Best Year Ever!** *seminars. These seminars have been inspirational, not only for me as a teacher, but for my students as well. Since adopting* **Best Year Ever!***'s proactive philosophy, I am amazed at the difference in both my teaching style and in the overall classroom atmosphere. I have become much more confident as a teacher, and look forward to each new year that awaits me. I feel blessed to have been introduced to the* **Best Year Ever!** *program.*

**—Margaret Hansen-Wood, 2nd Grade Teacher
White Pine Academy, Leslie, Michigan**

*Bill's attention to detail on the things that count in the classroom make this book a necessary item for all beginning teachers' desks. I would add that no matter how many years experience you have teaching, this book will inspire you to always make this year and every year the* **"Best Year Ever!"**

**— Richard Comar, Middle School Math Teacher
Detroit Public Schools**

*I began using the* **Best Year Ever!** *program in my third year of teaching. Before that, I had used a combination of strategies that just worked okay.* **Best Year Ever!** *has given me a foundation to my classroom management style. Everything else (curriculum, creativity) builds from there. It is something that gets me excited every year and brings students the power they have within themselves. It focuses on positive thinking, goal setting and, most important, a belief in self. Students are able to take the skills learned in my classroom and apply them to all areas of their lives.*

**— Laura Smith, 5th Grade Teacher
Waverly Community School District, Michigan**

*Bill Cecil's* **Best Year Ever!** *was one of the most practical and energizing presentations I have attended as a teacher. Bill's dynamic ability to relate his experiences with his message captivated my attention. I was able to use much of his TEAMS concept in my classroom immediately. I also began my classes the following semester, encouraging my students to have their* **Best Year Ever!** *by focusing on Bill's three components: Attendance, Attitude, and Effort. Identifying three simple yet essential components of a student's classroom responsibilities in such a way allowed for two things to happen: my students had three attainable goals on which to focus, and I had three areas to assist my students in improving. This combination helped to foster a positive classroom experience for all involved. As a new principal, I plan to implement these same concepts with my staff members and their classrooms.*

**— Timothy Fulcher, High School Math Teacher
Hazel Park, Michigan**

# BEST
# YEAR
# EVER!

## Winning Strategies
## to Thrive
## in Today's Classroom

**Bill Cecil**

**Best Year Ever! Press**
**Wheaton, Illinois**

**Best Year Ever!**
**Winning Strategies to Thrive In Today's Classroom**
by Bill Cecil

**Published by:** Best Year Ever! Press
Post Office Box 4176
Wheaton, IL 60189-4176 U.S.A.
Phone: 800-690-1233
Fax: 630-682-8933
E-Mail: BillCecil@BestYearEver.net
Website: www.BestYearEver.net

ISBN-13: 978-0-9779411-8-6
ISBN-10: 0-9779411-8-3

Library of Congress Control Number: 2006911189

Printed in the United States of America

0 9 8 7 6 5 4 3 2 1

# Dedicated to...

Those teachers striving to lead their teams to greatness!

# Thanks to...

My wife (Andrea), our son (Joe)
and
all my former students and teachers that I have had the great
pleasure of working with, and to the two greatest teachers in
my life—my mom and dad.

# ACKNOWLEDGMENTS

I truly believe that in life, no one reaches any great accomplishments totally on their own. In my case, I know that I have been blessed to have so many people help support, guide and cheer me on each time I set and go after the next big challenge in my life. Writing this book has been quite a challenge, and I know I couldn't have done it alone.

I must thank three very special people for their time, talent and patience working with me to transform my manuscript into a book that I am extremely proud to share with my fellow educators. The three people are Robert Aulicino (cover designer), Carolyn Porter of One-On-One Book Production (book designer and copy editor) and Alan Gadney of One-On-One Book Marketing (technical editor).

I have so many other people to thank as well. However, my fear is that when you start listing names you run the risk of leaving someone off your list. Therefore, I want to simply thank all of you who have taken part in this great journey, and I only hope I am able to repay you with the same love, support and encouragement you have given me.

Thanks!

# ABOUT THE AUTHOR

Ask Bill Cecil, a 20-year veteran teacher, what he loves most about teaching, and he will tell you very passionately that each year he gets to create, lead and be an active member of a "winning team." Bill believes every teacher is a leader with a team to lead, and he has created a program called *"Best Year Ever!"* that provides teachers with a clear vision, blueprint and proven strategies to create a positive, safe and productive learning environment where individuals strive for personal best while working together to achieve team goals.

Bill graduated with honors from Western Michigan University with a Bachelor of Science Degree. While attending Western, Bill earned four varsity letters playing on the men's soccer team and discovered his love of teaching while coaching youth soccer camps for the Broncos. Not only did Bill discover teaching through soccer, he learned the potential power a group of individuals have when they work together with a shared purpose or set of goals. He has incorporated those same team-building strategies into his own teaching with great success.

Bill was chosen **Michigan Teacher of the Year** for **2003-2004.** Bill spent that year on sabbatical working for the Michigan Department of Education setting an ambitious goal to meet with as many educators, legislators, community members and teachers in training as possible. He wanted to help spread an "epidemic of hope and determination" throughout the state of Michigan and the country, that now is a great time to be involved in education, we are all leaders with teams to lead, and that we have to first believe we can achieve before we can meet and master the many challenges we currently face in education today.

What motivated Bill to write this book is his deep concern that too many novice teachers are leaving this tough but rewarding profession before they have a chance to taste success in their own classrooms. He believes losing 30-50 percent of our new teachers within their first five years is a problem that must be addressed in order to help create a healthy environment where every child can achieve. Bill wrote this book to help reach as many teachers as possible with his winning management strategies.

Bill has earned a reputation for being a dynamic speaker that provides rousing presentations and workshops on classroom management, team building and leadership that are relevant, entertaining and loaded with practical ideas and strategies. For information on Bill's availability to speak to your organization or group, call 800-690-1233 or go to www.BestYearEver.net.

Bill resides in Mason, Michigan with his wonderful family and continues to teach for the Waverly Community Schools in Lansing.

# CONTENTS

# INTRODUCTION

Teaching is one of the most exciting, rewarding and fulfilling professions one can embark upon. However, teaching can also be the most grueling, time consuming, and stressful challenge you will ever face—especially when you begin your teaching career.

Don't take my word for it. Take a look at any number of statistics that track the success rate of our novice teachers; those who teach from zero to five years. Most statistics report the same startling fact: *somewhere between thirty to fifty percent of all novice teachers will leave the teaching profession within three to five years!*

It seems unbelievable to think that close to half of those who enter this profession will leave before they even have a chance to succeed in it. What other profession burns through its workforce as quickly?

I think the more important question is, "What are we doing or not doing to our new teachers that is forcing so many to run for the exits so quickly?"

Looking at some of the (apparent) reasons why our new teachers are leaving can be a bit misleading. Low pay seems to be a top reason many give, but I have a hard time buying that. Most pre-service teachers know long before they stand in front of their first group of students what teachers make or don't make. I don't think most teachers enter this field looking to get rich. Most are looking for the other rewards that teaching provides, like building positive relationships and feeling pride in knowing you have helped others to achieve.

No, I believe money *only* becomes a factor when you are not happy in this profession or not feeling successful as a teacher. I feel the number one reason why we are losing so many of our novice teachers within their first five years is because many are feeling isolated, frustrated, stressed out and unsuccessful in trying to do what they entered this field to do — Teach!

Unfortunately, I believe that much of this frustration is caused by poor induction and mentoring programs and a prevalent "sink or swim" attitude which still exists in our profession. As an analogy, imagine trying to teach a five-year-old to ride a bike by throwing her on a two-wheeler and shoving her down the biggest hill in the neighborhood, thinking, if she survives this, she will definitely know how to ride a bike! As insane as this may sound, we introduce many of our new teachers to teaching with this same approach.

I've heard experienced teachers brag that they "barely survived" their first year in teaching, but it did make them stronger. So therefore, they feel that everyone has to go through this rite of passage.

I disagree!

We need to provide training wheels for our young teachers so they can gain confidence in their abilities while they work to master the basics. Training in classroom management and relationship building should be the two main themes of professional development provided during the first years of teaching.

When it's time to remove the training wheels, we need to have people running along side of our new teachers to keep them balanced until they can move forward on their own.

Good mentoring programs can provide new teachers with that support—cheering them on, and picking them up when they fall. We shouldn't think of assigning each teacher with just one mentor, but rather a team of mentors who provide a safe learning environment in which to excel and grow.

Even though I strongly believe that the material covered in this book can help everyone involved in education, I am targeting this book specifically to the novice teachers who are beginning their careers. I am writing this book to act as a mentor and a set of training wheels for each new teacher who is just starting out. I will show how to build positive relationships with students and provide effective techniques to better manage students in the classroom. Thus, a teacher can spend more time stoking the flames of enthusiasm for learning, rather than wasting precious time and energy continually trying to put out brush fires of chaos and disorder.

I am going to introduce some powerful, proven strategies that will help those new to the profession not only survive the first years teaching but also will help them to thrive and enjoy! This book is not designed to replace any of the valuable training already achieved through college studies, student teaching, or classroom experiences. Think of this book as the training wheels that will support you until you are ready to ride on your own. Think of me as the guy running behind your bike giving you support and cheering you on. I will also be there to help pick you up, dust you off and help you back on whenever you fall.

I've broken this book into two parts. Part one will provide the four key strategies on which to concentrate during the first two weeks of the school year that will better prepare the children to learn. I call this section *Setting the Table for Success*. Too many teachers are in such a rush to serve the meal (teach the curriculum) that they fail to take the needed time to properly set the table (create a positive, safe learning environment for all students). I will show you how this little investment of time will pay you (and your students) huge dividends down the road, and will cut down on much of the frustration, wasted time, and stress many teachers and students unfortunately go through.

In Section Two of this book, I will provide a step-by-step *playbook* for how to create a "Best Year Ever!" experience for students and you teachers alike. This section will include lesson plans and activities to use with the students that will set them (and yourself) up for success. I'm confident that using this approach will drastically cut down on the waiting time to feel successful in the classroom and will even have teachers with more experience coming to you for ideas to improve their teaching.

Finally, as you read this book, I'm challenging you to find as many connections as you can to your own teaching situation. Every teaching situation is different. As you read, think about your grade level, your students, your students' needs and your individual needs. Don't think you have to do everything exactly the same way I do in order for it to work for you. Make any adjustments needed to make it work for you, and work to make this playbook your own by doing it your way.

Also, don't think you have to do everything I mention in this book to be successful. Take small bites, chew on it for a while, and once you feel you have mastered that bite, move on to the next chunk. Start small and build off each success. Take some risks, allow yourself to make some mistakes and learn from your mistakes. I'm twenty years into my career, and I'm still making mistakes, which means I'm still growing as a teacher.

Most important, remember that what you lack in experience you can more than make up with enthusiasm. Enthusiasm is contagious, and that is exactly what is needed in education right now. You are already bringing a lot to the table that makes you a valuable asset to our profession. The key is to never lose it.

My goal is that the following pages will help you keep that enthusiasm alive and provide you with strategies to become successful very quickly in your classroom so you don't become just another statistic as those who leave way too soon. So, turn the page, read on, and always remember, you have the power to make it happen—your **Best Year Ever!**

# SECTION ONE

# SETTING
# THE TABLE
# FOR SUCCESS

# Chapter One

# THE FOUR-STEP STRATEGY

Think of yourself and your students as a team. It's your responsibility to lead this team to success by creating a positive, safe and productive learning environment where individuals consistently work together to achieve team goals while striving for personal best.

In Section One, I provide a viable plan that you can use to help build your team. I call this simple, four-step strategy *Setting the Table for Success.*

Each year in my classroom, I invest time at the beginning of the year to "set the table" (build my team and learning environment) before I "serve the meal" (teach the curriculum).

Before I get too far ahead of myself, I want to discuss why I believe the team approach is important for teachers to use in the classroom, and why you must become a strong leader of your team if you want your team to become a winning team.

## Why the Team Approach?

A few years back, a DARE officer (Drug Awareness Resistance Education) talked to my students about how young people join gangs. He told them that he knew how it was done around the Lansing area, and that this method for being initiated into a gang was happening all over our country.

He explained that in order for someone to join a gang, he would have to place himself inside a circle of gang members. For ten minutes, this person wanting to join would have to endure punching, kicking, spitting and any other type of abuse the gang members could inflict on him. He couldn't fight back. He just had to take it. At the end of ten minutes, if he could crawl, stagger or walk out on his own without help from anyone else, he was in! He would then be initiated into the gang. The officer went on to tell my class that once you were in the gang, you were treated like royalty.

I was appalled at this story and did not believe it. I said to him, "How can you tell my class that story! There is no way that could be true!"

His reply to me was, "Oh, Bill, it's true!"

I said, "No way! What kid in his or her right mind would climb inside that circle knowing what was about to happen?"

He replied, "Obviously, many kids. Just look at how many gangs we have in this country."

I asked, "But why? Why would they allow this to happen to them?"

He explained that there are so many children who desperately want to feel a part of something larger than themselves that they are willing to risk their own safety and lives to be a part of a gang.

I worry that we are raising a society of lost souls. Of course, I am not suggesting that *all* our kids are growing up feeling disconnected or lost, but I do feel there are enough to be concerned about.

Too many kids have never had an opportunity to experience *even once* being a part of something larger than themselves — working with others to accomplish things they could never accomplish on their own.

As teachers, we have the power to give all of our students a chance to become a member of a winning team—a place where they can work with others to achieve team goals while pursuing their personal best. And, we can provide them with this opportunity in a safe, positive and caring learning environment.

People often want to belong to something larger than themselves. That's why so many people join churches, clubs, organizations, unions, groups and teams. As teachers, we have an awesome opportunity to create, lead and be a member of our very own winning team each and every year we teach—which leads me to my next point.

## Every Teacher is a Leader with a Team to Lead

Every great cause throughout history has had a great leader with a grand vision who was able to enlist others to join in that vision while providing them with a workable plan to get them where they needed to go.

◆ The Civil Rights Movement had Martin Luther King, Jr.

◆ The space program had President John F. Kennedy.

◆ India had Gandhi to help eradicate the caste system.

◆ The poor had Mother Theresa to help bring love, compassion and aid to their cause.

◆ Every great cause has had a great leader.

In education, who is our leader? Who is the one person we can all look to for that grand vision, who will enlist us all to join in sharing that vision, and who has a viable plan to take us where we need to go in order to create the great moment in education that people will be talking about for years to come? Who is our leader? I do not know who our leader is!

Unfortunately, we don't have the luxury of waiting for our great leader to arrive—especially with all the pressing demands and challenges that we face in education. Therefore, every single person involved in education *is* a leader with a team to lead!

Every person involved in education is a leader who must first lead him or herself, and then, more important, must lead a team. The vital questions each leader must be able to answer are:

◆ **Do you know where you are leading your team?**

◆ **Are you excited about where you are leading your team?**

◆ **Do those on your team know where you are leading them?**

◆ **Are they excited about where you are leading them?**

As a leader with a team to lead, it's crucial that you have a clear vision of where you want to lead your team. You must be excited about your vision if you hope to enlist your team to share in it with you, thus making it a team vision. Just getting to the end of the school year is probably not a good vision, because you're going to get there anyway. Teaching your curriculum may not be a great vision either, because it may be hard to get your team excited about it. You want to find something that will truly excite *you*—and your team.

Don't feel bad if you don't already have a clear vision. For many years, at the beginning of my career, I didn't have a clear vision of where I was leading my team. It's easy to go into teaching without a clear vision of where you want to lead your team, and once the year gets going it's almost impossible to find the time needed to think of a vision.

When I served as Michigan Teacher of the Year (MTOY), it was the first time in 18 years that I was not in the classroom. It gave me a great opportunity to view what we do for a living from the outside looking in. *I must tell you what I saw really scared me!*

What we do each year, and the pace we're forced to maintain throughout the entire year while doing it, is absolutely insane. Every day, from the minute we walk into school until we leave at the end of the day, we are running a sprint. And every day, from start to finish, we're wrestling with the clock! We're constantly fighting the clock trying to squeeze out as much time as we possibly can every single day for roughly 180 days.

Seriously, we go 120 mph all year long! We go 120 mph from August to June. Therefore, it's crucial that we go into each school year with a clear vision of where we want to lead our teams already firmly established. By going in without a clear vision of where you want to lead your team, you risk missing a small window of opportunity at the start of your year where you can grab your team's attention. Let them know *you're* excited about where you plan to lead them, and get *them* excited about where they're going.

The second thing to consider as a leader with a team is that all great leaders lead the way *they* want to be led. They model the way. Instead of wasting time and energy complaining about what other leaders have or haven't done to help you do your job better, lead your team the way you wish your leaders would lead you.

This is simple Management 101 - **MODEL THE WAY!**

A great thing about winning teams is that they attract fans. Lead your team the way you would want to be led, and I guarantee that your winning team will attract fans. Others will start approaching you to ask what you're doing to get your team to perform at such a high level.

Every year, I get quite a few parent requests to have their children placed on my team. I have a reputation in my district for being able to create winning teams in my classroom every year. I take great pride in that reputation and work hard to maintain it every year.

You'll be using some of the most common strategies that many strong leaders have effectively used in creating winning teams in many different industries. From the business world to the sports world, from the battlefield to the playing field, these common strategies have created many winning teams. By using many of the ideas and strategies in this book, I'm confident that you, too, will start to earn a reputation as a teacher many parents will want to have teach their children.

As you read through this book, you'll need to think of ways you can make adjustments when needed so that your plans will work most effectively with your team. If I've been able to take strategies from many winning teams and make them work with my fifth graders, I'm confident you'll have no problem making the needed adjustments to make them work for you.

Remember, every great team or cause needs a great leader with a grand vision, someone who can enlist others to join in that vision and can provide the team with a doable plan to take them where they want or need to go.

My doable plan, *Setting the Table for Success,* starts with the next chapter: *Strategy #1: Creating a Shared Vision.* My success formula is a four-step plan that will help you create a winning team that will attract many fans.

I focus on four things whenever I start working with a new team. I believe these four things can help turn *any* team into a winning team. Each year in my classroom, I invest the first two weeks in "setting the table" (creating a positive, safe learning environment and building the team) before trying to "serve the meal" (teaching the curriculum) to my students.

After the first two weeks, I continue to use these four strategies throughout the year, similar to how I take care of my car. About every 3,000 miles, I invest a little time out of my busy schedule to get an oil change to help keep my car running smoothly. I don't wait for the oil light to come on and my engine to burn out before deciding to get my oil changed. By changing the oil every 3,000 miles, I'm using preventative maintenance to keep my car running smoothly to prevent a major breakdown from occurring. I use these four strategies the same way to help keep my team running smoothly.

The four strategies I use are:

1. Creating a Shared Vision

2. Team Building

3. Teach, Model and Practice Team Procedures

4. Establish and Consistently Enforce Team Rules and Consequences

This detailed explanation of the four strategies, including techniques I use to implement each of them, will show you how to use them for your success and the success of your students.

# Chapter Two

# STRATEGY #1: CREATING A SHARED VISION

## The Leader's Vision

T he first strategy is what I call creating a team vision or a shared vision. But before you can create a shared vision, as the leader of your team, you must first create *your* vision. You must not only know where you want to lead your team during the school year, but you must be excited about where you want to lead them.

There is a quote I really like in Bill Parcels' *Finding a Way to Win*: "Winners develop a vision and enlist others to join them." Bill Parcels is a Super Bowl-winning coach in the National Football League (NFL). I've changed his quote just a bit to better define what I consider makes a great leader: "*Leaders develop a vision and enlist others to join them.*"

Having a clear vision is like having a target to aim for every year with your team. When I speak to groups of teachers, I sometimes ask them to imagine that I have a bucket of darts next to me and a target hanging on the back wall opposite where I'm standing. I ask them to imagine what would happen if I challenged a member from the audience to step up and throw as many darts as possible at the target for five minutes. At the end of five minutes, I will pay them $5.00 for every dart that hit the target. The darts wouldn't even have to hit the bull's-eye, just the target!

When someone takes me up on my challenge, I blindfold him, turn him around and around in circles, and tell him that I have moved the dartboard to a new spot in the room. I then tell him to begin throwing darts!

I'm sure you can imagine how hard that teacher would work during those five minutes, trying to hit the unknown target. He'd work feverishly to throw as many darts as possible in many different directions, hoping to hit the target at least once during those five minutes.

I'm sure you can imagine what the room would look like when I removed the blindfold from the exhausted and very frustrated teacher at the end of the five minutes. There would be darts everywhere—scattered on all four walls, the ceiling and even the floor. And maybe, just maybe, if the teacher was very lucky, a dart landed on or near the target.

To me, this is a good analogy of what a classroom with no vision looks like. There are many teachers working extremely hard in their classrooms, day after day, with no real vision or target at which to aim. Imagine that each dart scattered around this room is a student in a classroom with no clear direction, spinning out of control with his or her own agenda and energy.

Now imagine that I did this exercise again with another volunteer, but this time I do not blindfold the teacher, nor do I turn her around in circles or move the target. At the end of five minutes the room would look much different. This teacher would most likely work just as hard to throw as many darts as possible, but she would be much less frustrated during those five minutes. In fact, my guess is that she would feel successful at the end of the five minutes because many of the darts she threw would have actually landed on or near the target.

Even if not every dart landed on the target, they would be clustered a lot closer than in the first scenario. To me, this is a classroom with a clear vision. The teacher/leader of this team knows where she is going and is able to harness the energy of the team to get there—or almost there—much more consistently than can the teacher teaching in a classroom with no vision.

Again, it's important that as a leader with a team to lead you know exactly where you want to lead your team. It is equally important to make sure that you create a vision you can truly get excited about and that you can maintain that excitement for an entire school year. I can't imagine how leaders can inspire others to follow them on a journey *they* aren't even excited about.

Give this some good thought!

Where do you want to lead *your* team?

Every year I get to create, lead and be a member of a winning team. That's *my* vision! Actually, my vision is much more detailed and provides me with many targets to shoot for as I work to create, lead and build my classroom into a winning team each year. I would like to share my vision with you.

## Bill's Vision

I try to create a working environment in my classroom where:

◆ People truly care and show care for one another.

◆ There is trust among teachers, students and parents.

◆ There are no feelings of "Us vs. Them."

◆ All feel they have worth and respect.

◆ Spirits are high.

◆ Students work together to solve problems and generate new ideas to enhance learning.

◆ The positive environment encourages students to take risks and try new ideas.

◆ Mistakes are seen as a chance to grow.

◆ Students go out of their way to help other students because they feel confident and good about themselves.

◆ Pride shows through in everything.

◆ Students are happy and parents are satisfied.

That's my vision. These are the targets I aim for every year. I've been very successful in hitting the targets (or many of them) every year in my classroom throughout my career.

I have my vision written down so I can review it often during each school year. My vision isn't written in stone, because I consider it a work in progress. I'm still striving to improve my vision to become the best I can be as a teacher and leader in my classroom.

I'm often asked how I came up with my vision. I don't want to give anyone the impression that I just sat down one day with a pencil and paper and wrote out this detailed vision. My vision has been slowly evolving over the last twenty years. I've developed my vision by listening very carefully to others as they've described my room to me over the years.

I listen carefully to what guest teachers, substitute teachers, administrators, teaching peers, parents, former students, current students and others who happen to visit my classroom have to say about my team. Often they will tell me what they like about my team. I write their statements down and make sure they become conscious targets to aim for with my future teams.

If you're just starting out in the classroom or are struggling to come up with a vision of your own, take one or two targets from my vision to help you get started.

*Don't start off with too many targets.*

Remember, my vision *has taken me* almost twenty years to form. Start with one or two targets and learn to hit those targets consistently before adding new targets. It's better to start small and build off your successes than to bite off more than you can chew and choke on it. Too big a bite will only lead you (and your team) to become frustrated and confused about where you are headed. In this case, less is definitely more!

I see my vision for my team as the journey I will lead them on throughout the school year. The targets help me create my overall vision, which is to create, lead and be a member of a winning team. I believe those targets help me to create a positive, safe learning environment where individuals in my room can work together to achieve team goals while striving for their personal best.

## The Importance of Having a Shared Team Vision

Creating an exciting, clear vision for your team is only the first step in putting together a winning vision. Once you have *your* vision in place, you must start the work of making it a *shared* vision. You very well may have the greatest vision in the world mapped out for your team, but without taking the time to make sure it becomes a *shared* vision, trying to reach your target will be like trying to drive your car with the parking brake on. Even though you seem to be moving forward, it will take a lot more effort, take a lot longer to get where you are going (if you get there at all), and you will definitely feel resistance.

Miki, my oldest sister, and her family learned that valuable lesson the hard way a few years ago. Miki, like my family growing up, also has five kids. Her oldest child was about to enter college. As all her kids were very close in age, she knew that once her first child left the nest it wouldn't be long before they'd all fly the coop to start their own lives. She also knew that time was quickly running out to get the whole family to go on summer vacations together.

Therefore, she created the "mother of all visions" for her family's last big summer vacation. She envisioned cramming herself, her five teenage kids, their big old yellow dog, and her husband (not necessarily in that order) into a rented Winnebago and heading out west to see seventeen states in twenty-one days. Yes, seventeen states in twenty-one days! They were going to hit the city of San Francisco at the southern point, and then head north to Seattle, Washington to see my younger sister, Sarah, before heading back home to Holland, Michigan. It truly was the "mother of all visions!"

My sister was so excited about this trip that she got the rest of my family excited, too. I was so excited that I was in her driveway with my family on an early July morning, waving good-bye to her family as they started their incredible journey. We wished we were crammed in the Winnebago with them.

Miki was so proud of herself for coming up with this vision. She e-mailed us from the road, rubbing it in our faces about how great the trip was going.

> *"We are having such a great time! I can't believe how cool this is and how much fun we are having! I can't believe all the beautiful things we are seeing. Everyone is having so much fun! I have never seen my family closer. It is the greatest vacation ever, and I am so thrilled that I thought of it!"*

She went on and on, bragging . . . until about Day Five!

On Day Five, the e-mails started to take on a different tone. Storm clouds were forming on the horizon.

*"I'm not sure what's going on. I'm confused. So-and-So didn't come out of the van to see the biggest ball of wax, and So-and-So and So-and-So aren't talking to each other. I think the dog is sick, and the van is starting to smell. Everybody better start getting it together, because we still have a lot to see and a long way to go."*

By Day Thirteen, the e-mails became quite disturbing.

*"I HATE my family! They are so selfish!! Everyone seems to hate everyone right now, and nothing seems to be going well! We are so lost! I have no idea where we are, and I feel like we are never going to get home! I just want to get home! SOS! May Day! May Day! I want my mommy! HELP!"*

On Day nineteen, all communication ceased! I kid you not, I was afraid to turn on CNN in fear that I would see a helicopter chasing a smoking Winnebago down some deserted highway, with a news anchor saying that something had gone terribly wrong, and the station would keep the home viewers abreast of the situation!

When they finally got home, my sister swears that no one in her family was talking to one another. She even swears that the dog wasn't barking at anyone for a few days. And she has the photo history to help document this disaster.

At the beginning of the trip, you see pictures of family, love, togetherness, unity and beautiful sights. In the middle of the trip, the pictures showed factions starting to develop, not as many smiles, people missing . . . beautiful sights. By the end of the trip, the photos showed no people, just beautiful sights; and the pictures were blurry because they weren't even stopping the Winnebago anymore. They were just trying to get home.

I couldn't believe that this trip could possibly end so badly. She had formed such a great vision. I had even wanted to go on the trip. How could it have failed? I asked her what happened.

She told me that her kids had their own idea of how they wanted to spend their summer. Their vision didn't include being crammed into a tin can with wheels like a bunch of sardines for three weeks, traveling all over the country. Instead, she told me they would have much rather spent their summer making some money at their summer jobs and lounging around their pool with their boyfriends and girlfriends. That was *their* vision.

My sister's grand vision and her kids' grand vision clashed, because she didn't take time to create a shared vision. That's why many great visions fail!

Unfortunately, I believe this happens all too often in many of our classrooms and schools. Teachers are in such a rush to get to their creative lesson plans and to start teaching the curriculum, they forget to take time to set the table to assure their students are ready to partake of the year-long feast.

I even know a few teachers who are so excited to start teaching on the first day of school that after introducing themselves and taking roll, they then tell them to open up their math books and turn to page six while taking a quick look at their watch, impressed that they are already "teaching" ten minutes into the new school year.

These teachers often walk into the teachers' lunchroom the first day of school and brag about how they're already through chapter eight, wondering why everyone else is so far behind them. They strut around the lunchroom as if to say, "I'm *teaching* in my room, Baby! What are you doing?"

However, these also tend to be the teachers who, within a month or two, are openly complaining about their kids for the rest of the year. These teachers are convinced, year after year, that they are cursed with yet another defective group of kids who seem to be resisting or struggling with the great lessons they are trying to serve up to them.

These teachers are in such a rush to serve the meal that they forget to take time to set the table by focusing on these four strategies – the first strategy being take time to create a shared vision with your team.

## How to Create a Team's Shared Vision

By now, I hope I've convinced you, as a leader with a team to lead, how important it is to have a clear vision and how important it is to make it a shared vision in order to help set your team up for success. Now let's look at an easy-to-accomplish plan that can be used to help create a shared vision with your own team.

When you clearly know what your vision is and you feel excited about it, it's then time to share it with your team. You need to be realistic about your vision so that your team will share it with you. This is going to take some time and effort on your part.

Most visions don't sell themselves or become shared visions automatically.

I don't want you to think that I enter my classroom each year reading my detailed vision to my students and they look at me and say, "Yes, Mr. Cecil, that's our vision too! Let's go forth in perfect harmony to create a positive, safe learning environment where everyone will work together to achieve team goals while striving for individual best this year." Just like that I have "buy-in" from every member of my team!

Please! That is not the way it works.

We all need to find a more effective way to have our vision become a shared vision.

## Turn Your Vision into a Win-Win Situation

The key to success in creating a shared vision with your team is to demonstrate how your vision can help create a win-win situation for everyone on your team. For example, I explain the learning environment I am trying to create in my classroom each year. With my vision firmly in mind, I help my students envision all the benefits they can have if we can create that desired learning environment.

I ask them to imagine experiencing a school year in which they make friends that may last a lifetime. I then ask them to imagine a year where they learn to do things they never thought they could possibly do — where they can become confident that they can achieve anything for which they set their minds. I have them imagine a year that flies by, because each day they're finding many different things to get excited about and are having a blast being challenged to grow in many different ways. Finally, I ask them to imagine that at the end of the year they'll consider this one of their best years in school—if not their very best!

It is important to create a shared vision in such a way that your team gets excited about it — so that it becomes their vision. That's what good marketing campaigns do. They play up the benefits of what they are selling so that consumers want it—or, better yet, feel they *have* to have it.

## Rewarding Good Performance

An essential element of your campaign to transform your vision into a shared vision is to clearly define the pot of gold at the end of the rainbow — the one you and your team will be aiming for throughout the school year. They must know what's in it for them! It must clearly answer any questions they have about why they should buy into your vision and embark on the mission of making that vision a reality.

This is a great time to talk about the difference between extrinsic and intrinsic rewards. Both can play an important role in helping to turn your vision into a shared vision.

I always start with extrinsic rewards with my team and work toward intrinsic rewards.

There are people who don't feel comfortable offering extrinsic rewards in order for their team to perform better. I've heard them argue that they feel it's the same as giving dogs treats to do tricks (in other words, a bribe). I strongly feel it gives them something to aim for.

In fact, extrinsic treats motivate teams to perform better everywhere—especially in the sports and corporate worlds. In sports, world-class athletes are chasing after something that even their fame and fortune can't buy. They're chasing after a ring. Teams that win the World Series, Stanley Cup, NBA Championship or Super Bowl get one of these rings to wear for all to admire and envy. Players can't buy these rings (extrinsic reward) or the pride (intrinsic reward) that comes with wearing them. They have to earn the rings by outperforming all the other teams. That's what continues to drive many of these athletes to give their all.

I understand that corporations sometimes offer year-end bonus checks that individuals and teams can earn by reaching a goal or quota for the year. My brother, a corporate lawyer in Atlanta, assures me these rewards do indeed exist.

By the way, extrinsic rewards don't have to be hard to earn, nor do they have to be expensive, to be meaningful. Many of my teaching peers—and I—become excited when we get a handwritten note from district administrators telling us they appreciate the good work we are doing. Parents wanting their children to be part of your classroom is another reward to aim for. In our profession we don't receive bonuses, however, being appreciated means a lot.

Extrinsic rewards can serve as great incentives to keep a team motivated long enough to let the intrinsic rewards kick in. Two years ago, my team proved this to me by wanting to keep track of the number of hallway compliments received throughout the school year. Let me explain.

A few years ago, I was frustrated by the way many students walked down the hallways at our school. In an attempt to cut down on the noise they made, I often found myself closing my classroom door when other classes walked past.

As the year wore on, my door was closed more often than it was open. I hate having my door closed, because it makes me feel trapped in my room but, more important, I think closed doors in a school make the school seem uninviting. I turned down my first teaching offer because, when I was given a tour of the building where I'd be working, I couldn't help but notice almost every door leading into the classrooms was closed. It looked more like a prison under lock-down than a place where people shared ideas.

I decided I wanted my students to be the model for how people should walk through hallways without disturbing others. I offered my students an extrinsic reward that included five extra minutes of recess for each compliment they received for the way we walked as a team through our halls.

At first, my students were highly motivated to walk down hallways in a manner that would earn them extra recess time. However, it didn't take long for me to realize that the extrinsic reward was becoming less important than the intrinsic rewards they were starting to experience as a winning team. Winning teams attract fans, and my team was attracting attention from many of the adults in the building.

I knew the intrinsic reward of pride was becoming more important than the extrinsic reward of extra recess time as my team received more than one compliment a day, and they were excited even when the compliments didn't give them any more bonus recess time. In fact, they made a point of keeping track of all the compliments they were getting. They asked me to keep their running total on our chalkboard.

They went from wanting to earn extra playtime to wanting to earn a reputation for being a strong team of leaders in the hallway. They felt a special pride that meant more to them than the extra five minutes they were originally chasing. They earned forty-seven compliments by the end of that year—a number for which they took great pride.

That number became a record the next year for my next team of students to try to beat. I put "47" on an index card, explained what the number meant, and told them I was leaving it on a wall until another team beat it. That was all it took to motivate that team to start chasing the record. Though I offered no extrinsic reward, that team set a new record by receiving fifty-six hallway compliments during their year. My current team is on pace to break that record by year's end.  Pride in accomplishment can be the greatest reward.

Extrinsic rewards can also be used effectively at the start of the year to enable your vision to be shared.

Each year in my classroom, I try to get my students to adopt a shared vision where everyone works together to achieve team goals while also striving for their individual best. Our ultimate goal is to create a *Best Year Ever!* environment in which all the students can experience and take pride in.

I tell them that in order for *me* to have my best year ever, they must be able to have one of *their* best years ever in school. Therefore, as their leader, I will do everything I can to help them reach their goal. I use an extrinsic reward to define their pot of gold.

The pot of gold my team chases each year is an end-of-the-year cookout immediately followed by an entire afternoon of playing kickball with my teaching partner's team sometime during the last week of school.

That's it!

During the first few weeks of school, I market this reward to the point where you'd think this was a Super Bowl ring! I sell the idea until they truly believe they are the luckiest kids this side of the Mississippi.

My goal is to get them to buy into my vision long enough to start experiencing some of the intrinsic rewards that come with being on a winning team. I want to hook them long enough to start to feel what it is like to be a part of something larger than themselves, trying to accomplish things they may not be able to accomplish on their own.

Just how long does it take to market/sell a shared vision?

## Twenty-One Days to a Shared Vision

It usually takes twenty-one days to form or break a habit. Pavlov's dogs taught us this. They didn't just start salivating the first time Pavlov rang the bell. It took about twenty-one to thirty days to condition those dogs to slobber on command. I'm convinced that most diet and exercise programs work as long as people stick with them long enough to start seeing results, which takes about twenty-one to thirty days.

Unfortunately, many diets and workout programs fail because the people using them expect instant results and quit too soon. My guess is the people who have the most success with these programs stick with them long enough to start seeing results, which motivates them to keep going until, eventually, whatever they are doing becomes a habit.

It takes roughly twenty-one to thirty days to form a habit. I believe the same is true with creating shared visions. Although it takes twenty-one to thirty days to create a winning shared vision for your team, it doesn't have to take a lot of time on each of those days. In my classroom, I spend no more than fifteen minutes a day during the first month to create my team's shared vision, and about two to three minutes a day during the rest of the school year. I'm like a boxer, finding times during each day to jab away at my team, working on my vision to make it our shared vision.

If the boxer analogy is too violent for your taste, think of me as a peaceful gardener working diligently on my garden so the plants can grow to be strong and healthy. As anyone who has done any gardening knows, weeds don't need to be planted to grow in your garden. They show up uninvited and, if left unattended, can damage the plants you do want to grow in your garden. I like this analogy because it reminds me that negative thoughts are like weeds that can take root in our minds without us even planting them. As the leader of my team, it's my job to help eradicate any negative thinking that may be going on in my team, to plant as many positive images as I can in my students' minds to help nurture those thoughts to become strong and fertile.

As the saying goes, "What you focus on, you become." I work to get my students to focus on our vision and all the benefits our team will receive by working to make it a reality daily. As I'm teaching each day, I look for as many connections to our vision as possible—especially at the start of the year as I'm building my team. I know I've done my job well when my students start making these connections and sharing them with the rest of the team before I do.

An example that will help to explain this strategy better is something I call the "Quote of the Day." I have a huge collection of positive and inspiring quotes famous people have said throughout history. Each morning, before school, I write one of these quotes on the chalkboard next to our agenda.

When the students come in, I go over the agenda with them and read the quote that I've written down for the day. I ask them to take two minutes in their groups to talk about the quote and relate it to our team and our shared vision to have our "Best Year Ever!" After two minutes, I call on volunteers to share their interpretations of the quote and how it relates to our class working to become a winning team.

After I call on a few students, I share what I think it means and how it relates to our team. I then have everyone (including myself) write for three minutes in our journals reflecting on the quote. Next, I pair up students to read their responses to each other and then randomly choose three students to share their entries with the whole class. Last, I share what I wrote before getting on with our busy day.

This activity takes less than ten or fifteen minutes a day, but it's a powerful way to reset the table for success each morning with my team. It helps us to focus on our shared vision as we prepare to do our important work for the day, and includes a daily dose of writing. Usually, about 21 days from the start of our school year, students start bringing in their own quotes from home to write on the board. I know our shared vision is healthy and has a life beyond our team. It's not just our team vision any more; it's becoming a part of their life vision as well.

## Create Team Goals and Action Steps for Each Goal

Another way I help my team to focus on our shared vision daily is to have our team goals and vision hanging in our room on big yellow chart paper that is positioned on the wall opposite our door. It's the first thing you see as you enter our classroom. At the top of the huge paper, it reads, "Our Team's Goals."

About twenty-one days into the year—or after I'm pretty sure my vision has transformed into our shared vision—I ask the kids to help me map out three or four interim goals to reach along the way to our ultimate goal of having our "Best Year Ever!" I tell them this will serve as our road map during the year to make sure we are staying on target.

Instead of setting the goals myself, I have them work in groups to come up with the goals they think we need to achieve to make our vision a reality. From there, we share their ideas and check off goals that sound very similar from group to group. These goals will eventually be rewritten to make up our class goals.

While it may seem risky for me to allow my students to set the goals, it really isn't. The key is waiting at least twenty-one days, or until I'm sure they've bought into my vision and it has become our team's shared vision. By waiting, it's given me time to keep nurturing the vision and feed their minds on what it will take for us to reach our ultimate goal. I've shared the goals I think we should set many times without ever really referring to them as *our* goals.

When I do this activity with my team and they begin to repeat what I've been sharing all along, I act as if I'm hearing it for the very first time and think it's brilliant. Being patient, giving them time to take in my ideas and make them their own, and allowing them a chance to share with each other helps to insure they will choose appropriate goals. Consider how much more effective this is than if I had just dictated four goals and made them a class mandate for all to follow.

Below is a sample of a few class goals my teams have set over the years. What is amazing is that they do not vary much from team to team or from year to year and they sound very similar to my detailed vision that I shared earlier.

## Mr. Cecil's Teams' Goals

◆ Work well as a team and make sure everyone feels worth and respect.

◆ Give your best effort and challenge yourself to take risks this year.

◆ It's okay to make mistakes, but learn from them!

◆ Work to have your "Best Year Ever!" or at least have fun trying.

◆ Come to work each day with a positive, "can do" attitude!

Once we've established our team goals, we break each one down and create action steps that we can perform daily to help reach these goals. Goals without clear action steps are really just dreams. My team knows what we want to accomplish (goals) and has a doable plan (action steps) to use as our compass or road map as we embark on our year-long journey to make our shared vision a reality.

Earlier, I compared a team's shared vision to a target at which to aim. By posting our goals on big yellow chart paper, I provide a great visual aid that becomes the target we aim for throughout the year. Serving as MTOY, I had the great privilege of visiting many classrooms and schools. Although I saw a large number of incredible and inspiring things, I never saw a team's goals as clearly posted as mine are in my classroom.

I had to wonder whether the students in those classrooms and the adults in those buildings knew exactly where they were headed and how they were going to get there.

Think for a moment about the saying, "Out of sight, out of mind."

As the leader of your team, post your goals so all can see where you're leading your team and what your team is working to accomplish. And, once they're posted, refer to them often.

I refer to our posted goals often. I start the year off way across the room by the door and point to them whenever I talk about them. As we progress through the year, I stand closer and closer to our goals to represent how far we have come and how much farther we have to go to reach our goals.

As we reach the end of the year, I'm only steps away from our posted goals; but I never touch them. I tell my students to think about how far we have come during the year and how it would be a shame if we stopped short of attaining our goals. I tell them that the year has been like a long marathon, and that even though we can see the finish line, we must cross it in order to say that we truly reached our goals.

With my arm outstretched and the yellow chart paper just out of my reach, I warn my team that they may see some teams around the school starting to fall apart as the year winds down, but that we can't stop now. I urge them to stay on course and to stick together as a team so we can leave our room in June knowing we're the winning team we've worked all year to become.

On the last day of school, the only thing left on my almost bare walls is that huge sheet of yellow chart paper with the team's posted goals. I finally touch that paper as I praise my team for being so special and tell the kids that I will always remember them with great pride for the accomplishments they achieved.

It's not until after my students have left the classroom for the last time to start their summers that I take their goals down. I want it to be the last thing they see when they stop to take one more look over their shoulders at the year we shared together as a team. I want them to see those goals one last time as our championship banner.

There you have it: a blueprint to help create an exciting shared vision for your own team. Of the four strategies I suggest to be used to set the table for success with your team, this is by far the most important. It also happens to be the most complex. However, I'm confident that if you follow the doable plan, you'll be well on your way to building your team into a winning team, and you will attract quite a few fans as you become more successful.

The key to your success is to start small, with one or two targets, and to build off your successes.

*Don't feel that you have to follow this plan exactly the way I do.*

Like anything in life, take what works for you and work to make it your own. Play with this plan until it feels like a good fit for you and your team.

I close this section with one more family story to illustrate how to create a winning shared vision with your team.

This took place near the end of the summer when my son, Joe, was seven years old. The previous year my wife, Andrea, the leader of *our* team, had a grand vision for our family. She wanted us to go to Disney World the following summer for our next big vacation. Andrea felt Joe would be at that magical age where he would remember this trip for a lifetime.

You might think that this would be an easy sell to the family—a piece of cake—turning her vision into a shared vision for our family. Of course, Joe was a quick sell! What seven year-old wouldn't want to go to Disney World for a family vacation? However, selling me on this vision was not going to be nearly as easy.

I had no desire to go to Walt Disney World. I thought Disney World was a bad idea. To me, it sounded like an overpriced, overcrowded, and overblown amusement park—not to mention that I felt it was too long a drive from Michigan to Florida. Cedar Point seemed a better choice to me. It would be closer, cheaper, and—with all those roller coasters—a lot more exciting!

This could easily have been the death of my wife's grand vision but, like the great leader she is, she went to work to convert her vision into our shared vision. Over the course of the next few months she patiently and persistently marketed her vision to me.

Whenever we were with other couples, Andrea managed to work the conversation around to talking about family vacations and her desire to go to Disney World. To this day, I don't know if she preplanned this; but every couple to whom she mentioned Disney immediately started gushing about how great a vacation it was for their family and how we should really go. Most couples referred to their Disney World trip as their favorite vacation ever.

Knowing that it would take more than a few glowing testimonials from satisfied customers to persuade me, my wife initiated the second phase of her plan. Suddenly, in strategic locations around the house, I discovered travel brochures, magazine articles, and books telling me all about Disney World and providing enticing pictures. She even found a videotape about the excitement of vacationing at Disney World. It kept mysteriously popping up in our VCR.

Over a period of a few months, not only was she able to wear me down into sharing her vision, but I actually became excited about working to make this shared vision a reality for our family. Our family mantra became "Disney or Die!" She had me, hook-line-and-sinker, and with that important step accomplished, my wife launched into implementing her attainable plan.

Planning a trip to Disney World takes work. It's not as easy as jumping in the car and driving to the corner store to get a gallon of milk and a loaf of bread. It takes lots of preparation and planning. The more I studied how to plan a successful trip to Disney World, the more complicated it seemed to be. We needed to consider and plan where to stay (inside or outside the park), when to go to avoid huge crowds, how to get there, how long to stay, which parks within Disney World to see, and how to best finance the trip, to name just a few.

As the strong leader of our team, Andrea broke this massive undertaking down into simple steps and constantly reminded us of our shared vision. In addition, she did something very important to keep us moving forward whenever we started to lose sight of our vision. She took the time to remind us about the pot of gold at the end of the rainbow waiting for us. She asked us to envision what that treasure would feel like when we would be in Disney World, riding the rides and seeing the shows.

We survived all the planning and preparation and embarked on our big vacation. Unlike my sister's big trip out West, this trip was truly incredible. Not only did our son enjoy this trip, we all had a blast! Looking back at that trip a few years later, I'm still amazed at the time we had. This was our family's best vacation yet.

Besides having a great time, I learned something valuable about the importance of having a grand shared vision. I've always known you sometimes come up a little short when setting high goals for your team and yet can still be successful, but I learned from this trip that you can sometimes surpass your vision and experience something even better than you envisioned in the first place. Our family would never have experienced this if my wife had not taken the time to convert her grand vision into our team's shared vision!

The only thing more amazing than the trip itself was the way Andrea took her vision and worked with me to make it a shared vision. As the leader, she did many effective things to pull this off. First, she knew that in order for her vision to become a shared vision it would take time, persistence and patience.

She became a sales representative for her vision and marketed it slowly, over a period of time. Andrea knew this was a big-ticket item and that rushing to close the sale would only scare me off. She knows that, like most people, I can't stand pushy salespeople and that I like to "buy" rather than "be sold."

With help from friends, books and brochures, she was able to get me to form my own vision of this trip and think about the wonderful benefits we would gain. Finally, when the time was right, she closed the sale by getting my commitment to make the trip a reality.

Remember, creating a winning shared vision for your team starts with *you*. As the leader of your team, you must create a vision that excites you, and one that you will be willing to work on with your team to turn into a shared vision. Don't be afraid to dream big; then take the time to map out that dream into a viable plan that will lead your team to success.

# Chapter Three

# STRATEGY #2: TEAM BUILDING

You can't bring a group of people together and expect them to magically become a team. That makes as much sense as a carpenter piling a bunch of wood together in the hope that it will magically become a house, yet, that's the formula too many in education seem to follow. Too often people are thrown together, called a team and expected to perform without any team structure taking place.

Just as the carpenter needs to build the house to a plan, so must leaders build their teams using team-building strategies. Why is this so important? Because people tend to be nesters who build walls around their nests to feel safe, which makes it very hard for people to work together as a team.

I'm sure many are thinking, "Wall building nesters? What the heck is he talking about?"

I have not, of course, attended many of the staff meetings or sat in many of the lunchrooms of educators reading this book. However, I will predict that many of you sit at the same table with the same group of people more often than not. Am I right? I'll bet I am!

I'll also wager that many of you have attended meetings and conferences outside your building, planning to meet friends there, only to find that you arrived first and had the uncomfortable task of marking your territory by "saving seats." You put stuff down here and there—almost lay your body across the table—while screaming at the other people:

*"Saved! These seats are saved for my people! Keep on moving! These are saved!"*

We do that because we're nest builders. We feel safe in our nests, and we build walls around our nests to feel protected. I do it. When I'm not teaching or speaking I'm one of the quietest people you'll ever meet. Thank God for my wife and son! They're the social ones in the family and do most of the talking for me when I'm out of my nest.

Until I get to know people, I can be a bit shy. I'm like our cats. If someone rings the doorbell, I run upstairs with the cats, yelling, "Who is it? What's going on? Tell me when it is safe to come back downstairs." And thank goodness for Caller ID, or I'd never answer the phone.

Although most people probably aren't as extreme as I am, most people are nesters who build walls to feel safe—and it's not only adults who do this. The point I'm trying to make is that kids do it too! I know, because I see it taking place in my classroom every year.

I work in a building that consists of ten fifth grade classrooms and ten sixth grade classrooms. We have four feeder schools (K-4) in our district that feed my building with many of our fifth graders. On the first day of school, I don't have a seating chart for my students. I allow them to come in and sit wherever they want until I can get to know them and decide what seating chart will best serve the needs of the team.

It never fails that kids from the same feeder schools will come in on the first day of school and sit together at the tables I've set up around the room. I know this because when class starts I ask my students what elementary school they are coming from. I ask students from Winans Elementary to raise their hands, and all the hands at one table go up. I ask how many are from Colt, and all the hands go up at another table. The same thing happens with the Elmwood and View students. They know someone from the same former nest.

As the leader of your team, you must take time during the first two weeks of school to start tearing down walls and building up trust between the students from different schools. I know high school teachers sometimes hate to hear this, but you must take time to play with your team. If you don't like the word "play" then use the term corporate trainers use when they work with adults. They use "icebreaker activities." Call it whatever you want, but invent activities with your team in order to get to know each other — especially during those first couple weeks as you're working to strengthen your team.

Like most teachers who feel the constant pressure of not having enough time to teach, I had to be reminded of this a few years ago when I was invited to work with a group of actors at Jeff Daniel's theater in Chelsea, Michigan. Before I was allowed to teach my prepared lesson, the artistic director of the Purple Rose Theater, Guy Sanville, told me we had to play a game they always play as a team before they start any workshop, rehearsal or performance.

I have to admit I was a little frustrated. I had worked hard to prepare my lesson plans for the day-long workshop, and I felt this game was going to waste precious time and put me behind schedule from the get-go. However, Guy was paying me for the day, and I was not about to bite the hand that was feeding me. Reluctantly, I prepared to play the game with his team while keeping one eye on the clock.

The name of the game was Tape Ball. It is much like playing Hacky Sack, but without using your feet. The object of the game is to form a circle and randomly bat a ball of tape around the circle with your hands as many times as possible without someone hitting it twice in a row or the ball hitting the ground. The goal is to beat your highest score or the highest scores of those playing in other circles.

We played for ten or fifteen minutes before diving into my lesson. By the time I was allowed to start teaching, I felt as though I was teaching a group of friends rather than a bunch of strangers. Even though I was behind schedule I felt the group and I were very connected and I was able to move through my lesson at a faster pace than I usually experienced with other groups.

During lunch, I couldn't help but ask Guy why he insisted that we play that game before I could start teaching my lesson. He explained that there were several reasons, but the main reason that morning was because I was new to the group, which changed the dynamics of his team. Even though I was only going to be working with his team for one day, he felt it was important to take at least a little time to do some team-building so we were comfortable working together.

He explained that, in his business of putting on pro-fessional plays, he has to create a safe working environment where his actors can feel safe to take huge risks so they can put on high quality, entertaining shows for their paying audiences. In the world of professional theater, a company of actors has only a few weeks to prepare for a show. The actors must come into the rehearsal process willing to take huge risks in front of their peers in order to get their characters up to performance level in a very short amount of time. Guy told me that he can't afford to work with actors who are afraid to take big risks or make big choices, because the process would take too long and they would never be ready for opening night.

As I sat in the restaurant listening to Guy, it dawned on me how similar our responsibilities are. I, too, need to tear down walls in my room and start building trust so that every student begins to feel safer to take bigger risks in his or her learning.

Every teacher has students in the classroom who are afraid to raise their hands, for fear they may be wrong and possibly laughed at for making a mistake. Unfortunately, many of these students eventually feel disconnected from the rest of the team and may tune out. Worse, they may act out and become disruptive to the rest of your team.

As teachers, we need to work to create a positive, safe learning environment where every student can feel safe taking risks and making mistakes in pursuit of learning. We're in the business of creating positive risk takers. Playing games with your team can help to create that healthy learning environment where students feel safe taking risks in front of their peers.

As I said before, during the first two weeks of the school year, I find a little time throughout the week to play with my team. I find activities or games that will get my students moving around, away from their nests. I find activities that call for group interaction that includes working closely together to complete the task. I try to choose games that are easy to learn and a lot of fun to play.

To aide you in creating activities, I encourage you to read two books: *Tribes,* by Jeanne Gibbs, and *Cooperative Learning,* by Spencer Kagan. I also offer some team-building ideas in Appendix 1: *Quick Tips, Ideas and Activities.*

However, many of the ideas for the activities I use in my classroom come from outside the teaching world. They come from corporate training books and theater books that you can find at any major bookstore. The corporate training books are sometimes located on the top or bottom shelves in the business section of the bookstore because they are often oversized books. If you look for books in the theater/drama section, look for titles that have the words "games" or "playing" in them.

I've also found a few books in the games section of bookstores as well. Look for games that people can play at parties that you can easily adapt them to work in your classroom.

I have three reasons I play these games and activities with my students:

◆ They are great icebreakers.

◆ They model the way I run my classroom.

◆ They facilitate a caring environment.

## Icebreakers

Games serve as great icebreakers for strangers to learn to work together.

In my fifth grade classroom, icebreakers are great because they help my students to focus on winning, or on successfully completing a task. They get so wrapped up in playing the game that they don't care who they are working with in order to do well.

Many times the activities are set up in such a way they don't have time to look for familiar faces or friends to work with. Often, they are forced to grab the first person they can find to get the job done. They don't have time to look for someone who is the same gender or who has the same color skin. They just need others to win!

Later, when I team up students to complete certain tasks, they know they don't have a leg to stand on if they complain they can't work with certain kids, because they have already proven they could during the games. Actually, after playing these games with my new team, I hear very little, if any, of that kind of talk from any student. They've already proved to themselves they can do it and can enjoy doing it.

Icebreakers get groups touching and laughing within minutes. This helps to further tear down walls and build trust within the team. I often use icebreakers as an initial activity when I conduct workshops with teachers. I do this because I know that if I can get them up and moving and laughing early in the workshop, they will be much more engaged and receptive to the material I'm trying to cover.

Again, this is why corporate trainers earn big bucks to "play" with adults in the corporate world. While kids build walls around their nests, adults tend to build their walls much taller and much stronger. The trainers have to be able to dismantle these walls very quickly so they can get the adults involved to work together to solve problems and brainstorm ideas. Icebreakers help to increase productivity.

## Modeling Structure, Healthy Competition and Cooperation

The second reason I play with my team is that games model the way I run my classroom. Games are very structured, and so is my room. When playing a game, you must first learn the rules so you can play the game well. Not only do you learn the rules of the game, you learn the sequence of events that must be followed to keep moving forward in it. You learn what you need to do in order to pass "Go" and collect $200.

The same is true in my classroom. I have rules in my classroom that must be followed, and I usually have an agenda or a series of steps to follow to help my students get through assignments, projects and their school year with success. The sooner the kids learn how to perform within the structure I set up, the faster they find success playing on my team.

We're always pursuing clearly defined goals. I mentioned earlier that I post our goals in my classroom. We use them to help us achieve our ultimate goal—to have our "Best Year Ever!" Games model the same thing. Many games direct you to do several things in order to win the game. Kids know exactly what they need to do to win the game. They have a clear, shared vision and a doable plan, and they work with their teammates to get it done.

In a game, usually the team that can get it done first wins—which means teams are competing against other teams to get the job done first, better or both. Games are competitive and, believe it or not, there's a lot of competition inside my classroom.

However, I do not have students compete with one another individually to see who is the best or smartest, nor do I have my team compete against any other team in the building to see which class is the best class in the school.

Yet, my teams do compete to beat the records of my former teams. As I mentioned earlier, my current team is competing against a former team to beat their record for most compliments received in our hallways during one year. They're competing against a group of kids they've never met.

My current team is also competing against future teams of mine that have yet to be formed. They're trying to set records that future groups won't be able to beat. For example, we're keeping track of the days during the year when we, as a team, have had perfect attendance. So far, my team has recorded 40 days when we've all been in class out of the total 75 days we've been in school in our year.

They told me that their goal is to get to 100. Again, there is no extrinsic reward being offered for that number, but they want to accomplish it in the hope that none of my future teams will be able to beat it. I consider this healthy competition.

Games model cooperation, sending a strong message to the students that they need others to succeed in reaching individual and team goals. I look for games and activities that are designed so individuals can't win without the help of others. Theater books are a great resource for finding these types of games, because they're designed to help promote and build ensembles that will shine on the stage.

My classroom is set up the same way. We have learning partners and learning teams where kids work with others to complete certain projects and tasks. Even when students are working on assignments for individual grades, they may still need others to help complete their work. Students often mentor other students when they need help or have been absent. The goal is to create an environment where everyone keeps an eye on everyone else to assure that no one gets left behind.

Games model my personal philosophy in life, which happens to be *Highlights* magazine's mission statement: "Fun with a Purpose!" Games are designed to be fun, and yet they still have a purpose. Many individuals and teams play games, trying to be the fastest, rack up the most points, or both in order to win the game.

Games model exactly what I try to accomplish in my classroom. I work with my team to accomplish our team goals and shared vision while having fun. Fun isn't the engine that will drive my team to success. Hard work is what drives my team to success each year; but it's the fun we have as a team that keeps our fuel tank filled and keeps us working hard. It is fun with a purpose that keeps my team focused on and enthusiastic about the work we are doing.

Even though not every task we have to accomplish is fun, we can still enjoy working with each other to get the job done. As the leader of my team, I'm constantly on the lookout to find ways to make our journey together more fun, because I know I work harder and longer when I have fun and enjoy the people I work with. I'm not surprised that the same is true for my students.

In my career, I've been forced to work with people I did not enjoy on projects that were not fun. While I gave my best effort, I hated going to those meetings and was anxious to get out of there as soon as I possibly could each time we met. However, when I enjoyed the project—or at least the people I was working with—I found myself going early and staying late because I was having fun.

With this in mind, I'm determined to create as pleasant a situation as I can for my team as often as possible. I want my students to come in the door every morning wanting to be there, looking forward to our day together, versus kids dragging themselves in each day not wanting to be there. What a difference that can make in our day!

Two stories illustrate this fun with purpose theme. The first occurred during my year as MTOY. I attended a conference about the importance of using technology in our classrooms as a tool for learning. I was sitting at the table waiting for the conference to begin and was introduced to a professor from a college in our state.

When told next I was MTOY, she asked if I would be willing to speak to her college students about teaching. A few minutes later, I overheard her telling the woman she was sitting next to about the worst conference she had ever attended. It had been held some time in the '70s!

I couldn't wait to hear what happened at this conference 30 years ago that scarred her so badly she still can't let it go and feels the need to share it with others. She explained that a presenter had talked about how important it was for teachers to find ways to make learning fun for their students.

She became enraged again just talking about this three-decade-old event. She explained that she tells her college students that we should be teaching our young students that work is not fun but hard, and that they had better prepare to work hard the rest of their lives. Needless to say, I never called that professor to arrange to speak to her college class!

As a role model in my classroom, I want to show kids that as adults they can *and should* enjoy their life's work. Of course I don't enjoy everything about my job, but the day I start hating more of my job than I love, I'm leaving to find something I do enjoy. Life is too short not to enjoy what you choose to do for a living.

The second story took place a number of years back during a parent-teacher conference. A parent told me he had a bone to pick with me. Obviously, this was not the best way to start a conference. I asked this upset parent to take a seat so we could talk about his concern.

He sat down across from me, and started by telling me that his daughter seemed to be having a great year in my room. He told me she enjoyed working with me as her teacher, and she went home often talking about all the neat things we were doing in our classroom and about how much she loved school.

After five minutes of this, I must admit I was very confused. If this was a parent with a concern, I hoped all of my parents had similar concerns. I finally asked him what was bothering him because I still had no clue.

He told me that I was setting up his daughter for a major disappointment later in her life. He told me that I was teaching her that going to work each day can be a lot of fun, and that when she got older and started a career she would be disappointed to find out that going to work each day was not actually a pleasant experience.

Now I was really confused, and I asked him to go on. He told me that he hated going to his job each day and described in detail the many things he hated about his job. I waited until he was finished, then I respectfully told him how much I loved my job. I told him that the day I stopped enjoying teaching would be the day I stopped teaching. I told him I'd find something else to do with my life, because it wouldn't be fair to my students if I stayed.

In the end, I don't know if he agreed with me or not, but I do know his daughter continued to have a great year and many more after she left my class. I hope I was able to model to her that as an adult you can work hard and still have a lot of fun. I hope she also learned that people tend to work harder when they are having fun, because it is the fun that keeps them going strong.

## Facilitating a Caring Environment

The third reason I play games with my students early in the year is because I believe it forces everyone on our team to get to know one another more quickly. Forcing people to get to know others may sound extreme, but that is exactly what I do with my team when we start working together. I force students to get to know each other so they can start caring for one another quickly.

I have found that it's easier not to care about people you don't know than it is not to care about people you do know. I believe that the more you get to know people, the more you start caring for them and looking out for them.

If you leave it up to your students to get to know each other on their own, it very likely won't happen. Not everyone is social and outgoing, and many times people avoid going up to people they don't know if they have the option. I know this because I tend to be shy at first around people I don't know and usually don't initiate contact with strangers.

This must be as true with children as it is with adults, because I've visited other classrooms where many kids didn't know all the other kids' names in their room. How can you expect your students to work together as a team if they don't even know each others' names?

But don't think for a second that making sure everyone knows everyone else's name in your group is enough to build your team. I can't tell you how many committee meetings, graduate courses and professional development classes I've participated in where we were asked to start off by going around the room and introducing ourselves to the rest of the group. Too often, that's the extent of the team building that takes place before the meal is served and the real work begins. In many of these situations I knew just as much about the other participants at the end of our working relationship as I knew about them at the start—which, in many cases, was almost nothing.

Unfortunately, when people (especially adults) are thrown together but don't know much about each other, many in the group will remain very guarded and not feel comfortable sharing their knowledge or ideas with the rest of the group. This type of group may complete a task, but will most likely never reach its full potential, nor will the participants feel great about their overall experience.

In our rush to serve the meal we often skip this important team-building strategy so we can get to the "good stuff." As the leader of your team, you must force your team to get to know each other. Games are a great way to get this done in a non-threatening and fun way. However, games aren't the only way to build your team.

During the first two weeks of school, I have many strategies other than games that encourage (force) the kids on my team to get to know each other better. We conduct partner interviews where kids will be paired by my choice, given the task of interviewing each other, and then introducing their partners to the rest of the class sometime during the first two weeks of school.

I usually provide the interview questions to help the kids start out, but leave the activity open-ended enough that they are allowed to come up with their own questions as well. No one is forced to answer questions that may cause an uncomfortable feeling.

By spreading the partner introductions over a two-week span, it allows me to hold a few at a time each morning and afternoon, so my team doesn't start to find them boring. Twenty-something introductions in a row would be hard for almost any age group to sit through. This activity helps my team members become more comfortable getting up and presenting to their peers.

My teaching partner and I have our team of students interview us at the end of the first week of school. During the week, both classes put interview questions in a container. My partner and I bring both groups together at the end of the week and take turns reaching into the container, reading and answering their questions. Of course, we also have the option of not answering certain questions.

During the first two weeks of school, we have kids cut out magazine pictures of things with which they identify and arrange them into individual collages that represent them. Once the individual collages are completed, we arrange them into a large team collage in the hallway and title it "Identify our Identities!"

We explain to the students that the large collage represents our team—how we are made up of many individuals coming together with commonalities and differences. We explain that the commonalities are important—especially as we start to get to know each other—because it helps us connect with each other and feel more comfortable knowing we share certain interests.

We then explain that, as important as our commonalities are, our differences are even more important, because it will be the diversity on our team that will make us a much stronger team. The diversity that we each bring to the team provides more talents, skills and abilities we can pull from when needed to help us reach our shared vision and goals.

There are many different ways to build your team and many different resources to help you find the games, activities, and strategies that will best fit your team. The key to your success, as with turning your vision into a team vision, is to invest enough time—especially at the start of the year—to allow these strategies to work. The more time you take to build your team at the start of the year, the stronger your team will become.

Even after you build your students into a strong team, you must invest a little time throughout the year using team-building activities to keep your team strong. Think of this as getting an oil change. Just as car owners are encouraged to get their car's oil changed every 3,000 miles to help keep their car running smoothly, I encourage you to do some periodic team building to help keep your team working together smoothly.

Don't wait for the engine light to come on or for a major breakdown to occur on your team before taking action. Use team-building strategies as preventative maintenance to help keep your team on the road to success throughout the year. Think of team building as the quick pit stops you will need to make on your road to success.

I'm not a huge NASCAR fan, but I know enough about car racing to know that even the best-built cars need to make a series of pit stops throughout a long race if they hope to finish the race and possibly win it. These stops allow the pit crew to make sure the car has enough fuel and to make quick adjustments to the car to keep it running at peak performance until the next pit stop. Though many of these pit stops are scheduled even before the race begins, things will happen to the car during the race that will call for an unscheduled stop.

In my classroom, I have several scheduled pit stops planned for my team to help make the needed adjustments I feel will keep it performing at a high level for the entire year. I use team-building activities with my students to help us reconnect after long breaks such as our winter break in December and our spring break in April. Instead of expecting them to perform at the same level they were before the long break, I provide some team-building activities to help knock off the dust and get us back up to speed before resuming the curriculum at full throttle.

I usually change the seating chart in my room every couple of months so kids don't get bored sitting next to each other or start to drive each other crazy. This is another great time to schedule some team-building activities to get everyone comfortable working in new spots with different members of the team. Even though they've been in the same room during the year, there will be some wall building when kids are suddenly sitting next to new teammates.

One of my unscheduled team-building pit stops occurs whenever a new student is placed on our team during the year. Even one new student can change the entire dynamics of a team. It is worth a little time to bring the new student up to speed with the rest of the team as quickly as possible. The faster I can make that new student feel a part of the team, the better off the whole team will be.

I think of this as if I am managing a sports team and a new player is traded from another team. The sooner I can get that player to play well with the other players and to learn our plays, the faster that player will be able to perform well and help the entire team win. The same situation applies in my classroom.

As a final suggestion: When you work to schedule needed team-building pit stops into your year, make your team earn them. Often I play a team-building game with my students once, and they beg me to let them play it again and again. Though I know, as the leader of the team, how important these activities are to keep my team functioning well, I still make the kids think they have to earn them in order for us to play them again.

It's like getting your kids to beg you to take their vitamins or to beg you for extra vegetable portions on their plates. When you have your students earn things, they seem to become more valuable to them than if you just give things to them; and they work harder to get them. What a great win-win situation for you and your team!

# Chapter Four

# STRATEGY #3: TEACH, MODEL AND PRACTICE TEAM PROCEDURES

Take five minutes and make a list of all the procedures you have in place in your classroom to keep things running smoothly so that you can teach, and your students can learn. Go ahead and take five minutes—*right now*—to brainstorm your list.

My guess is that, if you really took the five minutes to complete this activity, you came up with quite a long list. As complete as your list is, however, I'll bet that if you had the opportunity to share your list with another teacher, you'd both probably find that you left off quite a few procedures from your list that the other had included.

It's always frightening to think how many procedures we have in our classrooms for our kids to follow each day to help keep things running smoothly. An even scarier thought is that of trying to teach in a classroom where the procedures you just listed are not firmly in place.

Someone once told me that teachers answer more than a thousand questions a day. I don't know if that figure is accurate, but I do know that, on certain days, the number seems a bit low to me—especially when you answer the same questions over and over, only to be asked them again and again.

Classroom teachers reading this know exactly the type of questions to which I'm referring.

*"What do we do when we finish our work?"*

*"Where do we turn in our papers?"*

*"Where do I put my field trip permission slip?"*

*"Can I get a drink of water?"*

*"May I go to the bathroom?"*

*"Can I go to my locker?"*

*"Can I sharpen my pencil?"*

*"May I use the phone to call home to get my homework?"*

*"Can I redo this for a better grade?"*

*"Can I use a pen on this assignment?"*

*"How long does my paper have to be?"*

*"What notebook do you want me to use?"*

*"Do I have to use cursive or can I print?"*

*"Is it okay if I chew gum in your class?"*

*"What folder should I put my math paper in?"*

*"Do we get recess today?"*

*"When is recess?"*

*"Is recess inside or outside today?"*

*"Where do we line up?"*

This is just a small sample of such questions. Questions like these are frustrating for teachers to continually answer because they're annoying, time consuming and usually asked at the most inappropriate times.

I can be in the middle of making a very important point in my lesson when a hand goes up and someone asks a question that has absolutely nothing to do with what I am talking about. You are in the zone, totally rocking and rolling through your lesson, when suddenly the momentum-killing question is asked, "When's lunch?"

There goes the zone!

Suddenly, you've lost your place in the lesson, and you've lost five or six other students who are now thinking about their empty stomachs. You feel like pulling your hair out and want to strangle the kid who asked that question. How rude!

As upset as you may be by that inappropriate question— and many more like it—it's a clear indicator that you have not taught a procedure well enough so your students no longer need to ask about it. Instead of trying to figure out when lunch will be served each day, they can focus on the lessons being taught if they *know* when it is lunch time.

Every day, we need our students to understand and follow multiple procedures in our classrooms so we can teach and they can learn. If we have to take time each day to answer inappropriate questions over and over again, we'll never get to the "good stuff."

Therefore, it's crucial to invest the time needed during the first two weeks of school to teach, model, practice and celebrate the procedures you want your team to follow the rest of the year. If you do this, I guarantee that the rest of your year will be a piece of cake. It really will be! And, you'll need to answer far fewer annoying and inappropriate questions.

My goal in the first two weeks of school is to break down my list of procedures and teach, model and practice a few each day until I can cross them all off my list. For example, by the end of the first two weeks, every student in my classroom knows the difference between when it's okay to get up and sharpen a pencil and when it's okay to get up and get a Kleenex.

I tell my students that they can never, *ever* sharpen their pencils in the room when someone else is talking. There are other procedures they can follow to get another writing utensil, and in a worst case scenario, they may have to just sit there until the person talking is through, but they can never, *ever* sharpen a pencil in our room when someone else is talking.

Why? Because it is rude, and no one will ever do that to them when they are speaking in our classroom. Now, if they have something hanging out of their nose, they should get up immediately and get a Kleenex because that's disgusting and can distract the speaker more if left unattended.

As crazy as that may sound, these are actually two separate procedures I teach, model, and practice the first two weeks in my classroom with my students. However, what's nice is that, for the rest of the year, I'm not battling the sharpener whenever I'm trying to teach, and no one in my room will try to sharpen a pencil when we have a guest speaking to our class.

I have many other procedures to teach, model and practice during the first two weeks of school with my team.

This is a partial list of the procedures I try to cover:

## Procedures Covered in Mr. Cecil's Room

◆ Walking in the hallway as a team

◆ Where to put lunches and musical instruments

◆ Where to put notes from parents

◆ Where to turn in permission slips and school forms

◆ Where to turn in redone assignments

◆ What to do in the classroom before we officially get started

◆ How to fill out agenda books each day

◆ How we take and turn in our attendance and lunch count each day

◆ How and where we line up to switch classes for Math and Science

◆ When students are allowed to go to their lockers during the day

◆ Bathroom procedures

◆ Recess procedures that include boundaries and rules for playing outside

◆ Where we line up coming in from recess

◆ How long students have when coming in from recess to use their lockers, go to the bathroom and get water so they aren't marked tardy

◆ When and how we use the classroom phone

◆ How and when we feed and water classroom pets and plants

◆ When it is the best time to raise your hand during a lesson to ask questions

◆ How we prepare to leave the room at the end of the day

◆ Filling out our daily homework/assignment books

◆ Sweeping the floor and putting up chairs for our custodians

◆ Passing out notes at the end of the day

   I have many more procedures in my classroom, but those I've listed keep me quite busy during the first two weeks of school as I work to make sure that every child understands them and knows when and how to perform each one with ease. The time I spend the first two weeks teaching, modeling and practicing these procedures is time I save the rest of the year *not* having to re-teach them on a daily basis. This time saved from answering many of the same questions over and over again gives me more time to teach—and far fewer headaches.

I always shake my head when I hear other teachers publicly bashing their students in the teachers' lounge. This is something that my teaching partner and I make a pact to *never* do. As leaders with teams to lead, how can we build trust on our teams if we're backstabbing them to others? This is something we just can't afford to do. We need to model the way!

I know that not everyone has this pact, because I sometimes hear other teachers publicly complaining about their teams. They make comments about how poorly the kids are behaving or how disrespectful they are as a group. I often hear comments like, "I can't even get my kids to walk down the hallway without running!"

I might say something like, "Have you taught them?"

They usually get upset and reply, "Taught them? They're sixth graders! They should already know how to walk down the hallways without running! You should have taught them how to do that in fifth grade!"

Here's where a breakdown occurs too often in our classrooms and schools. Too many leaders assume their students should already know how to do many of these things. They don't take time the first two weeks to teach, model and practice these important procedures with their team, or they quickly brush over them in a rush to start serving the meal.

Yes, I expect my kids to be able to know how to walk down hallways properly by the time they get to fifth grade. However, I can't expect them to know exactly how I want it done. Every leader leads his or her team a little differently. Therefore, it's only fair that we take time to teach, model and practice the procedures we want our newly formed teams to follow so they can learn what our expectations are and how best to live up to them.

Think about it. One of the first things every branch of the military teaches new recruits is how to walk as a unit. This is also one of the first things I teach my students. I don't teach them how to march down our hallways, but I do teach, model and practice my expectations for walking down the halls of our school as a team.

By the end of the first two weeks, my students clearly understand that when we walk as a team down our hallways no other class will have to close its doors because of our noise level, nothing will have to be reattached to the walls after we pass, and we'll all stick together as a team from point A to point B. We practice this enough the first two weeks so that it becomes a natural way we walk down the hallways for the rest of the year.

As with any procedure, you can easily go back and rework it with your students if you feel it's becoming a problem for your team. I believe most problems I hear other teachers complain about could easily be fixed if they'd only be willing to invest the time to teach, model and practice the procedures they want their kids to follow.

One of the most important procedures I address with my team involves conflict resolution. You can teach, model and practice procedures to deal with conflict on your team so it doesn't interfere with your team's shared vision or goals.

No matter how well you build your team, you can still expect a certain amount of conflict to exist. Sooner or later, every team will have conflict and will have to deal with it. Winning teams know how to deal with conflict quickly and in a positive way so it doesn't waste precious time or drain energy from the team. The more often the team deals with conflict, the less time it has to achieve its goals.

With that in mind, I use the first two weeks to introduce the *"Eight Modes of Conflict Resolution"* I learned from my all-time favorite education book, Spencer Kagan's *Cooperative Learning*. In this book, he introduces eight ways that any team can use quickly to resolve almost any conflict.

As the leader of many different teams, I've used these eight techniques just as much with adults as with children to resolve conflicts quickly when they arise and to help avoid future conflicts. Don't be fooled by their simplicity.

## Spencer Kagan's Eight Modes of Conflict Resolution

◆ Share

◆ Take Turns

◆ Compromise

◆ Chance

◆ Avoid

◆ Postpone

◆ Use Humor

◆ Get Outside Help

I post these eight strategies in my classroom for all to see. During the first two weeks of school, I introduce these strategies to the kids as procedures they will use when conflict arises on our team. I take time to teach, model and practice using these with my team, so that by the end of two weeks they will be able to use them competently for the rest of their year.

My goal is to train my students to use these techniques so that they'll resolve the majority of their conflicts on their own without having to bring me in to resolve them. Whenever I have my students begin work on a group project in my room, I first have them take two minutes to decide which three of the eight techniques they will use to avoid and solve conflicts when they arise.

I tell them to make me their fourth choice (Get Outside Help) with the understanding that when they come to me to solve their problems all negotiations are off, and they must be willing to live with my resolution. They can't hear what I offer and then decide to go back and use one of the other techniques they like better. I do this to discourage them from blowing past their first three choices to solve their problems just to get to me.

I believe it's better for the kids to decide which conflict resolution techniques they'll use as a team if needed before their group gets started on the project. It's better to get their plan in place while they are cool and collected instead of asking them to do this task in the heat of the battle.

I'm always amazed how well these eight strategies work to help keep my team running as a cohesive group. I'm not the only one. Other adults comment often on how well my kids work together as a team and in smaller groups.

My favorite story happened one day when a teacher came into my room during the last half hour of my teaching day to discuss a problem he was having. My students were busy working in small groups around the room, trying to finish projects they'd been working on, so I used this time to listen to this teacher's concerns.

About fifteen minutes later he was feeling better about his problem and was preparing to leave my classroom, when it dawned on him that my room was filled with students working busily together on projects around the room. He couldn't believe that during our fifteen-minute chat not once were we interrupted by any of my students, or that I needed to stop to redirect them. He was also amazed that with only fifteen minutes left in their day they were so focused on their work.

What amazed me was how amazed he seemed to be. I didn't see this as an incredible event occurring in my classroom, but rather saw it as my team simply performing procedures we'd practiced during the first two weeks of school to help us better reach our shared vision and goals.

Be sure to include these *"Eight Modes of Conflict Resolution"* in your team's procedures, and be sure to take time at the start of the year to teach, model and practice them with your team so the kids become more successful throughout the year to resolve conflicts as they arise, and avoid unnecessary conflicts whenever possible.

To read more about Dr. Spencer Kagan and cooperative learning, I suggest you check out www.kaganonline.com. It has information on many of his books, products, seminars and magazine. I believe this is a resource every leader with a team to lead should use.

# Chapter Five

# STRATEGY #4: ESTABLISH AND ENFORCE TEAM RULES

Though this fourth strategy for setting the table for success is important for a winning team, I believe it's the most important strategy for our new leaders and teachers to master if they have any hope of a lasting career in this tough profession.

This is the deal breaker! This is the foundation on which you will build your entire year. If you don't master this strategy, everything I've written up to this point will be of no use to you. Instead of creating a winning team, you'll be creating your own personal nightmare—and a nightmare for every unfortunate member of your team.

A team without clearly defined rules and consistently enforced consequences is a team destined to fail and to fail often. As a leader with a team to lead, your first priority always should be to protect your team and keep its members safe. If you don't provide a positive, safe environment or playing field for your team to work on, you're creating nothing but chaos! If you have chaos, you have nothing but a wasted year.

What kid in his right mind is going to take a risk and raise his hand in a room in which he feels unsafe, knowing he will most likely be teased by his teammates? No team can thrive if it's stuck in survival mode. It's imperative that you immediately establish clearly defined rules and consistently enforced consequences if you want to create a safe environment for your team.

My brother's family recently got a beagle puppy named Bingo. Philip took Bingo to dog obedience school. He shared with me that he was surprised to learn that dog obedience school is really designed to train the dog handler or owners more than it's designed to train the dogs. The dog owners are trained to be consistent with their commands, punishments and rewards so they can have a well-trained dog.

This is exactly what leaders need to be able to do consistently with their teams. They need to be clear and consistent in communicating what the expectations and rules for being a member of their team are, and they need to consistently enforce the positive and negative consequences depending on how well members of the team follow those rules.

To stay with the dog analogy, a few years ago some neighbors installed an invisible fence for their dog. When they first told me about this invisible fence, I thought they were pulling my leg. What's the purpose? How can a fence possibly keep a dog in the yard if it's invisible?

They explained that the fence is actually a series of cables that are buried underground around the border of the yard to mark off the area the dog owner wants the dog to stay within. These cables continually send out a signal when the power is turned on. The dogs are given a special collar to wear that will give them a slight shock whenever they step over the hidden cables.  This zap lets them know they are stepping out of bounds, and reminds them what the boundaries are so they will learn to stay within them.

At first, the dogs will test the boundaries several times in the hope of expanding them so they can have more room to play. If the owners are consistent with keeping the collar on the dogs and keeping the invisible fence turned on, the dogs will eventually tire of getting zapped and will stop testing the set boundaries. They learn to play within their given space. I was told that eventually the fences no longer need to be turned on because the dogs are so well trained.

No, I am not advocating putting special collars on our students so we can zap them when they overstep the boundaries we establish in our classrooms! Wouldn't the media have a field day with *that* story?

Seriously, I share this story because during the first two weeks of school it's crucial for teachers to establish a clear set of rules (boundaries) and to consistently enforce the consequences (zaps) so everyone in the room knows that there are set boundaries to respect and stay within.

Kids will test the boundaries, especially during the first two weeks of school, to see what they can and cannot get away with. This does not make them bad kids. They're simply trying to figure out the structure in your room and how it works. They want to know if it is more or less consistent with other teams they have played on, and how it relates to their family's structure or lack of structure.

I've often been described by my students as being "firm, but fair" and "fun." I like these three descriptors because I pride myself on running a very tight ship, which helps to create a positive, safe learning environment where we, as a team, can have fun.

However, the kids who struggle the most with my style of management usually come from less structured environments where they have more lax boundaries than those I've established in my room. I need to understand this and be patient with them. I also need to be tough as nails, because they're going to test me with everything they've got to see if they can beat me down into letting them do whatever they want, whenever they want, for the rest of the year.

This is a battle no leader can afford to lose if he or she wants to be respected by the entire team. Therefore, I must be most consistent at the beginning of the year while establishing my rules and consequences to send a clear message that I'm a strong leader with an even stronger will who creates a positive and safe learning environment in which all can thrive.

I'm in no position to tell you what rules and consequences you should establish for your team. That's up to you and your school district to decide, but I'll tell you that there are a few guidelines to keep in mind as you make these important decisions.

## Guidelines for Rules and Consequences

◆ Implement five rules (or less) that are easy to remember and easier to follow.

◆ Discipline with dignity.

◆ Use positive and negative consequences.

◆ Every day is a new day for everyone to have a fresh start.

◆ Focus more on the positive behaviors than on the negative behaviors in your room.

Although I believe all the guidelines are important to consider as you set your rules and consequences for your team, I believe the one you can't afford to overlook is disciplining your team with dignity.

If I'm going 80 miles per hour in a 70 miles per hour zone and get pulled over for speeding, I know I deserve a ticket. I may not want the ticket, but I know it's a law I chose to break and that, therefore, I deserve the ticket.

However, what I don't deserve is to be yanked out of my car and berated and embarrassed in front of my family and other drivers on the road before I'm given the ticket. I deserve just the ticket.

The ticket is my zap. I'll be sufficiently upset with myself for speeding and having to pay the fine so I'll most likely not speed in the future. Regardless of how I feel about the ticket, I expect the police officer enforcing the law to treat me with respect.

That's how I try to enforce my rules and consequences in the classroom. I let the consequence be the zap. Even though my students may get upset about the consequences they receive for their poor choices, I try to stay calm and positive by letting them know I am still rooting for them and working to help them succeed in my classroom.

For example, in my classroom a child will lose a full recess if she breaks three rules during any given day in the classroom. The child will usually be upset about losing recess for the day. My job is to let her know I understand that she's upset, and that tomorrow I'll work with her to earn back recess by being able to follow the rules more consistently.

I also try to spend as little time as possible focusing on the negative behaviors of my team and focus more on the positive behaviors. It usually takes me less than thirty seconds to discipline someone.

I may say to someone who's talking out in class, "Jimmy, I'm going to put your name on my pad for breaking our Rule #3. You need to remember to raise your hand. I know you can do this. By the way, that is your first reminder for the day." That's it. I'm finished, and I jump right back into teaching.

My goal is to give the child as little negative spotlight in my room as possible so that I don't embarrass him or give him the impression that you need to make poor choices to get attention in my room. It's my understanding that some kids thrive on negative attention, because that may be the only attention they get at home. I don't want that unhealthy behavior to exist in my room, so I work to give negative behavior as little attention as possible, without ever ignoring it.

Later, I may go out of my way to put the spotlight back on that child for making a more positive choice. I may say, "Jimmy, I really liked your response, and by the way, way to go with remembering to raise your hand. I'm proud of you. Keep it up!"

In my room, I try to focus more on the good than the bad without ever looking the other way when someone breaks our rules. I want my team to know that I'm diligent in making sure I keep our learning environment positive and safe for everyone all the time.

This *really* can be the deal breaker about how well you'll be able to lead your team and teach in the classroom. You can't expect to be successful without having clearly defined and established rules and consistently enforced consequences to help protect your team and keep it safe.

This doesn't apply only to kids. Adults need discipline as well. That's why we have laws to help govern our society and keep it running smoothly. Leaders of adult teams need to have the courage to discipline their teams when needed. If not, just like kids, many adults on a team will test the boundaries to see how much they can get away with doing or not doing.

I once was at a staff meeting where a teacher stood up and started swearing at another staff member attending the meeting. This teacher was out of control and out of line. Everyone else in the meeting sat stunned as he verbally attacked the other teacher—until the teacher being attacked picked up his things and walked out of the meeting.

What happened next was even more shocking. After the teacher being attacked left the meeting, the attacking teacher sat back down. There was about thirty seconds of uncomfortable silence—and then the meeting continued as if nothing had happened!

The administrator witnessed this attack but did nothing about it. When I asked why, I was told that everyone on the staff knew that the offending staff member just needed to blow off some steam sometimes, and that he usually regretted doing it afterwards.

Bottom line: I believe the administrator was as afraid of this bully as was everyone else on the staff. Unfortunately, this leader's lack of courage to discipline his team sent a bad message to the rest of the staff. It said that he was not there to protect his team and to keep the working environment positive and safe.

It was no surprise when people stopped sharing as much in future meetings because they didn't want to be unfairly attacked by this bully who now had free reign to do as he pleased. I don't think anyone would argue that this held the team back from reaching its full potential that year and years that followed. Not only did the team not reach its potential, but the overall morale on the team was hurt.

Leaders must have the courage to lead their teams and to keep everyone on the team feeling safe so they can continue to take risks to grow as individuals and as a team. It takes courage to stand up to bullies and other people on the team who are holding it back from trying to achieve the shared vision and goals set by the team.

Maybe that's why we currently have a lot of managers and not enough leaders in leadership positions.

I'll say it again: It takes courage to be a leader and lead your team. As a leader with a team to lead, you'll have many people looking to you to help create a positive, safe learning environment where individuals can strive for their personal best while working to achieve team goals. The success of your team will depend on how close you come to reaching your shared vision and team goals.

These four strategies can help you set the table for success with your team so that when you're ready to serve the meal your team will be more than ready to partake in the feast.

Now that I've provided you with a workable plan to help build your team into a winning team, I want to stress, one more time, the importance of taking the time that's needed to build your team. You can't rush this formula for success!

Think of this doable plan as a recipe for making your favorite cookies. Even though I've provided you with all the ingredients to make some fine-tasting cookies, they won't turn out if you don't mix the ingredients together and give them plenty of time to bake. This is one step in the process you can't afford to rush, though you may feel pressure to start serving the meal. Wait until the cookies are done!  Believe me, it's worth the investment of your time.

I'll finish this section by sharing one more story with you. It is about the first time I shared these four strategies I call "Setting the Table for Success" publicly with other educators. This was in St. Louis, Missouri in the summer of 2000.

I was unveiling *Best Year Ever!* at a character education conference to see if there was any interest in my classroom management program. It's hard to be a prophet in your own land, so I felt St. Louis was far enough from Lansing, Michigan to take that risk.

During my presentation, I stressed the importance of taking the first two weeks to set the table before trying to serve the meal by taking time to build the team and the positive, safe environment in which you want your team to perform before trying to teach the curriculum. The presentation seemed to be going quite well. People were taking lots of notes, and everyone seemed to be interested in what I was sharing.

At the end of my presentation a very polite first grade teacher, who had taught for twenty-seven years, raised her hand. Her name was Laura (changed name to protect her privacy), and she had more of a comment than a question.

Laura started by telling me how much she loved *Best Year Ever!* and how much she liked the four strategies I had just covered to help build a winning team. However, she went on to explain that she felt she could not afford to invest the first two weeks of her school year to "set the table."

Laura told me that in Missouri teachers are under a lot of pressure to prepare their kids to take state tests and to cover the state-approved curriculum, and that she just couldn't afford to give up two weeks to focus on the four strategies.

I told Laura that in Michigan we have the same pressures to prepare our students for state tests and to teach to our state-approved curriculum. I told her that I felt these four strategies, once established in her classroom, would help her get that mission accomplished, but I also gave her an out and told her I understood that what I just shared may not be for everyone. She mentioned again how much she liked what I had just shared, but still sounded concerned about the two-week investment of time I was asking her to make to build her team. When we finished talking, I was happy she liked my ideas but didn't expect her to follow through on them.

I didn't give that conversation another thought until the following May, when Laura called me at my home to talk to me. She said she had to tell me something. I was afraid she was about to lay into me about how I ruined her year and got her fired or something to that effect. Why else would she be calling me?

To my surprise—and great relief!—she'd called to tell me how well her school year had gone with her team of first graders. Laura told me that in her twenty-seven-year career she had never gotten further into her curriculum than she had that year. She said she felt she was seven weeks ahead of where she usually ended. I was happy about how excited she was, and asked her what made the difference. She told me the biggest difference she noticed that year was that she got to teach every day instead of wasting time trying to put out brush fires.

Of course, I had to know how she went from crowd control to teaching every day and what allowed her to get seven weeks further than in any year before, so I asked her. She said that what really made the difference, in her opinion, was that she had invested time during the first two weeks of school, as I had suggested, concentrating on setting the table for success with her new team.

Laura used those two weeks to concentrate on the four strategies I've just shared with you. Her investment paid off big time for her students and for her. I can't promise that if you follow this doable plan that you, too, will get seven weeks further into your curriculum than usual . . . but I'm very confident that as the leader of your team you will have to put out far fewer brush fires. You will have more time to teach and to lead your team to success.

Here is a checklist that will remind you of what needs to be done to help build your team into a winning team.

## Setting the Table for Success Checklist

### The Team Leader's Checklist

1.   Realize that you are a leader with a team to lead.

2.   Know where you are leading your team.

3.   Motivate and enlist your team to go with you by taking time to create a shared vision with your team.

4.   Lead your team the way you want to be led.

5.   Get your team members to believe they can achieve.

6.   Tell and show your team that you care about them consistently with your words and actions.

7.   Create a caring community through a team approach where individuals work to achieve team goals while striving for personal best.

8.   Take time to build and maintain your team.

9.   Teach, model, and practice the procedures you want your team to follow.

10.  Establish and consistently enforce team rules and consequences.

# SECTION TWO

# A YEAR-LONG THEME THAT FOCUSES ON TEAM

# Chapter Six

# OVERVIEW OF
# YEAR-LONG THEME

I hope after reading Section One, *Setting the Table for Success,*
you now have a better understanding and appreciation for
the need to invest time at the start of each school year to
build a winning team in your classroom. Even though I'm
confident the four strategies described in Section One will help
you become very successful in this tough profession, I'm sure
many of you are thinking:

*This all sounds great, but how do I do this on my own? How do I
get started, and where am I going to find the time to plan all this out
when I already don't seem to have enough time in the day to get
everything I have to get done completed?*

That's what this part of the book is for.

Instead of wasting a ton of time and energy, not to mention
stress, trying to reinvent the wheel by coming up with your
own effective classroom management program, I invite you to
use the blueprint I've spent years developing and continue to
use in my classroom each year to ensure that both my students
and I will have a truly special year. Keep using it until you have
more time and experience under your belt to develop your own
winning plan.

Unfortunately, too many of our new teachers are forced to
enroll in the 'school of hard knocks' in order to gain valuable

experience and figure out what strategies work in the classroom by first learning what strategies *don't* work. This is not only unfair to our novice teachers, it's unfair to their students as well. This frustration, I believe, is what drives many of our new teachers away.

By sharing this successful classroom management program with you, I'll drastically shorten your learning curve to success by providing you with a detailed playbook that will have you "setting the table for success" minutes after walking into your classroom the very first day of school, and will show you how to keep your team going strong until the final bell rings marking the beginning of summer vacation.

However, before deciding whether *Best Year Ever!* is right for you (and your team), take a few minutes to read through the overview below to get a better feel for what this program is all about.

Over the years, I developed my teaching style to be more like a supervisor and coach, constantly trying to find new ways to motivate my students to perform at a higher level. I created strategies and activities to use in the classroom to help match my style and, hopefully, better reach my students.

There are two major themes in this program. The first major theme comes from one of my all-time favorite books, Napoleon Hill's *Think and Grow Rich*.

*Best Year Ever!* stems from a simple—yet powerful—philosophy described in his book: *"Whatever the mind can conceive and believe it can achieve!"*

*Best Year Ever!* is designed to help all students experience their best year ever in school by planting a seed the very first hour of the very first day of school that says no matter what their past school experiences have been, this year can be their best yet!

You'll be able to guarantee your students will have one of their best years ever—if not the best—by committing to learning and doing three things on a daily basis throughout the year. The three words that hold the key to their success during the year are: *attendance, attitude* and *effort*.

The second major theme of this program focuses on turning any classroom into a caring community. Using the same philosophy that many of America's best companies use — *Treat your employees (students) like they are #1 and they'll respond that way!* —you can build a successful team that has *high morale, infectious enthusiasm* and *increased performance*.

By creating a *shared vision* (that includes a commitment to making every year your best year ever), you can eliminate problems that may be holding your students back from reaching their full potential!

Imagine working in an environment where the following are firmly in place:

◆ Trust between teachers, students and parents.

◆ A place where people truly care and show that care for one another.

◆ No feelings of "us vs. them."

◆ Everyone feels they have worth in the classroom and feels respect.

◆ Spirits are high.

◆ Students are working together to solve problems and generate new ideas to enhance learning.

◆ Positive environment that encourages students to take risks and try new ideas.

◆ Good ideas and outstanding performances are recognized.

◆ Mistakes are seen as a chance for growth.

◆ Students go out of their way to do a little extra for other students because they feel confident and good about themselves.

◆ Pride shows through in everything.

◆ Students, families and guests immediately notice something special when entering your classroom ... a "warmth."

◆ Make satisfied parents and happy students.

◆ All share the same vision.

I believe using the *Best Year Ever!* program will help you and your students in the following areas:

◆ The way you work as a team

◆ Setting higher expectations for all students

◆ Creating customer service second to none

◆ Job satisfaction

◆ Creativity/cooperation/growth

◆ Building a reputation as an outstanding teacher

The *Best Year Ever!* program is divided into three subjects. They are:

### Building an Individual's Mind-Set for Success

I'll help you introduce *Best Year Ever!* into your classroom on the first day of school, even before you have time to take attendance and introduce yourself. I'll show you a unique way to start your year off on a very positive note. Within minutes after walking into your classroom for the first time, your students will know they have stumbled onto something very special.

In this section, I'll take you step by step through the process of getting every child in your room committed to doing what it will take to have their best year ever and confident that they can make it happen!

By the end of the second day, you'll have set the course for every student in your room to have a truly remarkable year. They'll know that you care for them, that this is an opportunity for a fresh start to become whatever they choose to become, and that you'll be their biggest supporter along the way.

I know this must sound almost too good to be true, but by the end of day two, I can pretty much guarantee that your students will race home to tell their parents they are going to have their best year ever! You can imagine how excited your students' parents will be to see their kids this excited about the upcoming school year.

## Creating a Caring Community Through Team Approach

If the first two days of school are designed to help plant the seeds of success in each student's mind, this section will help you create a healthy garden in which they will grow. This section introduces the model, philosophy, rationale and techniques that will allow everyone to reach their personal best while working together to achieve team goals.

I'll share some strategies and ideas that will help you build a team that will make coming to work each day a joy. While other teachers are constantly working to put out little brush fires in their room, you'll be stoking the flames of enthusiasm that will be raging in your class. Other staff members will find working with your team a pleasure, and will swear you must have won the lottery by getting all the "good" kids in your room.

You will discover how using "Target Talk," "Environment," "All Involved," "Model Management," and "Service" (**TEAMS**) more effectively in the classroom will help to create a caring team that will make everyone's year—including yours—more enjoyable and memorable.

## Quick Tips:
## Ideas and Activities That Promote *Best Year Ever!*

In the Appendices, I'll share specific ideas and activities that have been "teacher tested" and "kid approved." Most of the strategies in this section are easy to learn and take little time out of the day to use, but produce big results if used consistently during the year. The ideas and activities can be easily altered to fit individual teaching styles.

The ideas and activities are listed in alphabetical order. However, I've provided a key at the beginning of the section explaining when best to use each idea and activity in relation to your school year.

*Best Year Ever!* can stand on its own, or it can be plugged into almost any other program to help make it even better. The same is true with individual teaching styles. *Best Year Ever!* is basically another set of tools to put into your backpack of teaching strategies. Put in only what works for you and what you think will work for your students.

Again, I'm providing you with the blueprint I use each year to help build my winning team in my classroom. Feel free to use all (or some) of this blueprint as you work to develop your own over the next few years.

In the meantime, I'm confident that after reading and consistently using this program, you'll be able to create a learning environment in which the students know you care about them and that their past doesn't equal their future. You'll create a cohesive group of individuals who will work together as a team to enable everyone to reach for their personal best—and hopefully have their **Best Year Ever!**

Chapter Seven

# DAY ONE: THE KICKOFF

## THE SPEECH

This is the speech that should kick off the *Best Year Ever!* program and help each student start building a mind-set for success. I use this speech to introduce my vision with my team and start working to make it a shared vision. I have broken the speech down into six parts that could be given all at once or throughout the day depending on your students' age level. The time this takes is 30-45 minutes.

> **NOTE:** Obviously, I don't expect anyone to memorize and give this exact speech in order for it to be effective. However, I wanted to include it to serve as a reference to the main points needed to be covered. I definitely encourage putting this into your own words to better match your style.
>
> Ideally, this was designed to be presented the first thing on opening day of the new school year. This will help to start your program. You can also wait to start it at the beginning of a new marking period, first day back after New Year's Day, or any other natural break in your school year.

## THE SET UP:

1.  Set up a sign to greet your students as they enter the room that welcomes them and instructs them to find a seat, sit down, relax, breathe and get ready for a great year. This allows you the opportunity to greet students (and their parents) out in the hallway and help any lost students to find their classrooms.

2.  After everyone has made it into your classroom, walk in with a big smile on your face, closing the door behind you.

3.  Speak to them as if you are telling them something *very* important, so that they will not want to miss a word of it.

4.  Speak slowly, pausing in selected spots to let what you are saying sink in.

## PART ONE—THE OFFER

Walk silently to the middle of the room and, without even so much as a "hello," "welcome," or "good morning," start the speech as if you are picking up right where you left off from an earlier conversation with them—like you are old friends just having another chat.

> *"Imagine that a person comes up to you and offers you a chance to have your best day ever! You would have a day full of fun and surprises. It would be a day where nothing would go wrong. This would be the perfect day that you'd never want to end. How many of you would be interested in such a day? Raise your hands if you'd be interested."*
> (Usually, all hands shoot up.)
>
> *"Now, imagine that same person comes up to you and offers you your best* year *ever! A year that would include lots of laughter, good times, exciting challenges, tremendous growth and fond memories. It would be a year that would fly by, and at its end you would look back and say, "Wow! What a year!" How many of you would be*

*interested in such a year? Raise your hands."* (Again, all hands go up.)

Take a moment to look at each and every student, and then say:

> *"Well, today is your lucky day because I'm that person and I'm offering to you—right now—an opportunity to have your best year ever.*
>
> *"I'll give you a school year you'll never forget. If you've had great years in the past, that's wonderful. Then this will be another great year. I don't want to push out any other great teachers or great years you've had. I just want you to add this one to the list.*
>
> *"However—if, for some reason, you haven't really enjoyed school in the past . . . this is your lucky day because this will be the year your feelings about school will change. I'm that confident in my abilities as a teacher that I can stand here and know in my heart that I can help you have your best year ever—or one of your best years ever.*
>
> *"IF ... "*

## PART TWO—THE CATCH

IF ...

> *"IF? I know what you're probably thinking right now. 'I knew it sounded too good to be true—best year ever. There's always a catch! Nothing in this world is free.' Am I right?*
>
> *"Well, you* **are** *right. There is a catch! In order to have your best year ever, you must promise or commit to doing three things for me this year.*
>
> *"That's it.*
>
> *"Three things.*

*"The good news is that these three things you must promise to do in order to have your best year ever are easy to learn and easy to do.* However, *you must do all three things to be successful. You can't choose your two favorites and leave one out. All three things must be done—and done well—to have your best year ever."*

Again, I'm dragging this out a bit to let the anticipation build.

*"I can guarantee you that you'll have your best year ever—or one of your best years ever—if you learn and practice these three things—three words—consistently all year long!*

*"Guaranteed!*

*"So listen very carefully because the next three words I say are going to enable you to have your best year ever. They are:*

*"Attendance . . . Attitude . . . and Effort!*

*"That's it—attendance, attitude, and effort."*

I walk over to the three words taped to a wall in the middle of my classroom and point to them as I continue.

*"That's the catch. That's all you have to do—to learn and practice these three words on a daily basis—and I promise to do the rest so that at the end of the year you will look back and say, 'That was my best year ever.'*

*"Now, before I ask each of you to commit to these three words, I want to quickly go over each word with you to make sure we have the same understanding of what it means and what I expect to see you doing this year to have your best year ever."*

I spend the next ten to fifteen minutes going over each word, defining it and modeling what a student looks like without using that word, and then with using it. You can't be afraid to be too big here! I'll overact each scenario so there is no doubt that my message makes clear what I'm looking for.

Also, by making your role-playing big, it remains entertaining while you have the kids sitting so long trying to absorb so much information—which, hopefully, will keep their interest long enough while you get your important message across.

Finally, one more reason I make this huge: I want to set the tone for the whole year in this short amount of time. During the next few minutes, I will make it clear to these kids that my classroom is a place where I feel comfortable to take risks, and that I approach my teaching/work with a lot of fun, full of energy and passion.

While most other teachers are busy passing out materials and taking attendance, my kids are awake and listening. I continue:

### *Attendance*

> *"The first word you must learn and master this year in order to have your best year ever is attendance. Of the three words or things to do, this is probably the easiest. All you have to do is come to class. That's it—just show up!*

> *"You have to have good attendance this year. You have to get yourself here on a regular basis to have your best year ever. You can't have your best year ever if you don't show up. Think about it. Michael Jordan, without a doubt the greatest basketball player of all time, could never have helped lead the Chicago Bulls to winning six NBA championships if he just sat on the bench all the time bragging about how good he was. First, he had to step out*

*onto the basketball court each season to have any hope of having his best year ever each year. You have to do the same thing by coming to class on a regular basis to give yourself a chance.*

*"The reason it's so important to show up on a consistent basis is so you don't fall behind or feel out of sync with the rest of the class.*

*"When I was a kid, I can remember wanting to stay home from school on certain days—usually days I knew I didn't have my work done—and when I went back to school the following day I felt out of sync with the rest of the class. I felt even further behind, which made me want to stay home even more.*

*"The more you miss, the harder it is to feel a part of the group, because when you come back from being gone, your classmates aren't in the same place they were when you left. Life went on while you were home watching reruns on the couch. It's not a good feeling. You can avoid it by coming to class.*

*"Challenge yourself to break your own personal record for least number of absences in one year. If your attendance record is already good, keep it going. Become the next Cal Ripken. Who's Cal Ripken? Who can tell me who he is and what record he holds in baseball?"*

It's worth pointing out to the kids that Ripken's record for perfect attendance – playing in consecutive games – was 2,632 games spanning over 16 years.  His record for perfect attendance would still beat their record if they could not miss one day of school from the time they started kindergarten to the day they graduated from high school. Pretty impressive!

*"Attendance is important, but understand that there will most likely be a few times you may need to miss because*

*you're really sick or you have a doctor's appointment. That's okay. Again, I'm asking you to do the best you can to show up this year. Shoot for your best record.*

*"Does anyone have any questions about attendance? Then let's move on to the second word you need to learn and do in order to have your best year ever."*

### Attitude

*"The second thing you need to do this year in order to have your best year ever is to have a strong, positive attitude. It's essential that you walk into class each day expecting something good to happen — looking for things to get excited about.*

*"Even the way you sit should express or encourage a positive attitude. You should sit up with both feet on the floor ready to go. Your face should have a smile on it or at least not a frown.*

*"Here — let me show you what I mean. First let me show you what I hope I don't see."*

I quickly exit the room and re-enter, slamming the door and grumbling out loud about how I hate school and everything associated with it. I'll have a look on my face that basically says, "Don't mess with me!" As I make my way to the back of the room, I stop along the way and get into someone's face and say, "What are you looking at?" Then I slam myself down into a chair and put my elbows on my desk to help prop up my head — still grumbling about my rotten morning.

I keep this up until I get a few giggles from the students and then I snap at the one closest to me, saying something like, "Shut up! It's not funny!" I'll then finish with a little more grumbling before I break character and become myself again.

*"You laugh. But believe me, I've seen students actually do that. When I see that, I already pretty much know what kind of day they're going to have. Oh . . . here's something else I see even more than that. Watch."*

I quickly bolt out the door, full of energy, and re-enter like a lifeless slug—no energy at all! I make my way back to the same empty seat with no expression on my face whatsoever and melt into my chair. I sit there a moment, lifeless, with my head starting to bob forward and back a little as if getting too heavy for my neck to hold up any longer. I rest my chin on my palms while making a heavy sigh. After another moment, I rest my head on my arms, and take it to the next level and actually rest my cheek on my desk like it's a pillow, expressing even louder sighs of boredom.

You can't be afraid to exaggerate this a bit. I've been known to take this a step further and crawl into the fetal position on the desk with my thumb in my mouth. It definitely gets the point across!

Once off the desk, I say:

*"You're laughing; but I'm telling you that, unfortunately, I've seen that one more than the other example I just showed you. I mean, I could be up here juggling fire and some students would still give me that attitude as if to say, 'This is boring.'*

*"I'm going to let you in on a little secret. Your body usually reflects your attitude—your body will act like a mirror showing how you're feeling inside. If you have a poor attitude, you'll most likely be frowning or looking bored. Right? I mean, it's really hard to keep smiling when you feel rotten inside.*

*"Now, here's the really cool part. Your body can actually control your attitude. You can actually change how you're*

*feeling by the way you walk, sit and which expression you put on your face. For example, try feeling rotten inside while walking or sitting up straight with a big smile planted on your face. You can even try saying negative things while doing this, and it still won't work. Watch. I'll show you what I mean."*

I stand up straight and walk proudly around the room with a huge smile on my face and say negative things to people, like,

*"I'm really angry. I don't like myself. I don't like you. I hate school. I'm bored."*

I'll break from that character and, as myself, say:

*"It's impossible to stay angry, bored, and unhappy, when your body is telling your brain something totally opposite. Therefore, it's important that you walk in each morning and sit at your desk each day in such a way that your body will help you feel positive."*

I then walk out and re-enter the classroom with a smile on my face and a skip to my step. I smile at my students as I make my way to my chair. I sit down and sit up, still smiling. After about a minute or two I say,

*"This is easy to do, and it will help make a difference this year—possibly enough to make it your best year ever.*

*"By walking in each day looking for something to get excited and happy about, you'll be amazed at how many things you'll find. By focusing your brain on looking for things to get excited and happy about, it will search like a computer to help you find what you're looking for. We'll talk more about this later.*

*"The second part of attitude is belief in yourself. You have to believe you can achieve whatever you set your mind to*

*accomplish this year. There's a book by Dr. Wayne Dyer,* You'll See It When You Believe It. *This book has a strong message that basically says you have to believe you can do something before you can actually do it—like every time Michael Jordan stepped out onto the court, he had to believe he could make the big shots when needed. You have to believe in yourself!*

*"The next time you think you won't be able to do something, keep this in mind: If you want it badly enough, you'll find a way to get it. Look at what you accomplished the first five or six years of your life. You learned how to walk, talk, read and ride a bike. Not one of those accomplishments are small. They're* huge. *And* you *did them! You were able to accomplish these huge feats because you wanted to do them so badly you had no room in your brain for a negative attitude telling you you're not good enough.*

*"You had a strong desire to do these things, so you tapped into your natural positive attitude to help you believe you could do them and then go out and do them. That's the same attitude you'll need this year to have your best year ever."*

### Effort

*"The third thing you have to do this year in order to have your best year ever is to simply try. That's it, just try. Not try to be perfect.* Just try. *You have to give effort.*

*"To better explain what I mean by effort, I want to tell you about one of my personal heroes. His name is Thomas Edison. Without Thomas Edison's effort we'd be sitting in the dark right now. We wouldn't have video games, TV, DVDs or iPods. He invented all these things—or their ancestors—plus many, many more.*

*"Thomas Edison was able to invent many things because he would not give up until he got the results he wanted. He*

*wouldn't stop trying. The light bulb took more than* 10,000 *tries before he got it.* Ten thousand! *Not ten tries or one hundred tries—more than* 10,000 *tries. To me, that's amazing! It also reminds me that if you really want something badly enough and you don't quit trying—most likely you'll get it.*

*"One last thing I want to tell you about Thomas Edison that made him so successful: He wasn't afraid to make mistakes. He didn't see mistakes as failing. He believed that making mistakes was necessary in order for learning to take place. He believed that each mistake brought him one step closer to reaching his goal. He believed that failure occurred only if you didn't learn from your mistakes or when you quit trying.*

*"I'm going to tell you something right now that I want you to remember the rest of this year. I don't expect any one of you to be perfect. I'm telling you that it's okay to make mistakes this year as long as you try to learn from them. Doesn't that feel good? No pressure! You don't have to be perfect, and it's okay to make mistakes. I also want you to know that this rule includes me, too. I'm not perfect, and I'll make mistakes.*

*"So, the next time you're wrestling with a math problem or you don't understand something I'm trying to teach, relax and think about Thomas Edison and the light bulb. Keep trying and don't give up—because you may only be one mistake away from success.*

*"That's it.* Attendance, attitude, and effort—*master these three words this year and I promise you'll have a year to remember."*

## PART THREE—THE COIN

I continue:

*"Attendance, attitude, and effort—that's all you have to do to have your best year ever or one of your best years ever. Every year, I set a goal to have my best year ever. I've been pretty successful with that goal because I consider last year my best year ever, the year before that was my best year ever, and I know that if I focus on my attendance, attitude, and effort, that this will also be my best year ever.*

*"This is so important to me that I had a coin made up to serve as a reminder to me that I have the power to make this my best year ever—and every year my best year ever."*

At this point, I pull out my coin and show it to the kids. I ask them to pass it around the room while I discuss everything on the coin. I want them each to get a chance to look at it closely and feel its weight. By doing this, I am hoping to pique their interest in what I am saying and hopefully create a desire to want one for themselves.

*"Here—I'll pass it around the room so you each get a chance to see it up close. Please be careful when passing it around because it means a lot to me."* (This gives the coin more value by asking them to be careful with it.) *"While you're passing the coin around the room, I'll talk about what's on the coin and what it stands for."*

I draw a picture of the front of the coin, and then describe each part.

*"On the front of the coin, I have the words,* **Best Year Ever!** *This is my personal goal. It reminds me that as a teacher I can make each year better than the year before. I can keep learning and trying new things to make me grow and keep my enthusiasm for teaching at a high level. It also reminds me of the goals I've set for you individually and for us as a team. I want all of you to have your best year ever, and each day I come to work I remind myself that's what we're working together to accomplish.*

*"The shining light bulb represents Thomas Edison's perseverance. It took him more than 10,000 tries to invent the light bulb. He never gave up, and by learning from each mistake, he eventually reached his goal. This serves as a strong reminder for me to never give up if I really want to accomplish something. The light bulb also represents the word "challenges," to me because Thomas Edison was always working to invent something that would make our lives better, and many times people told him he was crazy to think such things could be created. He enjoyed each challenge of trying to prove these nay-sayers wrong—and it's what kept him going. He wasn't going to let anyone else determine his limits.*

*"The words,* **Make It Happen!** *remind me that this isn't a lucky coin, but rather a 'make your luck happen' coin. I have the power to make my goals a reality by using the ideas/concepts covered on this coin. I don't live my life hoping to get lucky. I wake up each day knowing that I can go after any goals I set for myself, and the harder I work for them the quicker I'll reach them. It also reminds me of how important it is for me to help* **you** *realize that you have this same power within you so that when you leave my class at*

*the end of the year, you'll have the tools you'll need to make every year your best year ever."*

I draw the back of the coin on the board and quickly review the three words already discussed.

*"The word, 'attendance,' reminds me that I have to be here to have my best year ever. I can't help you have your best year ever if I'm not here. So, on those rare mornings I wake up feeling a little tired, I still make sure I get out of bed and get to work. It also reminds me that for you to have your best year ever, you have to do the same thing. By being here on a consistent basis, you will feel caught up and feel a part of the team.*

*"The word, 'attitude,' reminds me that if I walk into work each day looking for something good to happen—I'll most likely find it. It also tells me I can achieve whatever I set my mind to accomplish as long as I believe I can do it—even if others don't think I can. The same is true for you."*

*"Finally, the word, 'effort,' reminds me to keep trying and to never give up. I can make as many mistakes as it takes to reach my goals as long as I'm willing to learn from them so I don't keep repeating them. The word 'effort' also reminds me that the difference between wishing for something and making it happen is* effort. *When you give effort toward something you want—rather than just wishing for it—you have a much better chance of getting it.*

*"I want to share a true story, something that happened to me that helped me believe that everything on this coin has the power to make a huge impact on your life, if you just live what's on the coin.*

*"When I was a senior in high school, I was at my soccer awards night, and our coach started talking about who he felt would be able to play in college. He didn't mention my*

*name, which crushed me. I respected his opinion a lot and this came as quite a blow to me.*

*"I remember getting enough courage to confront him about this the next day, hoping that maybe he made a mistake and left my name off the list by accident or forgot to mention it. When I asked him, he told me he honestly didn't see me having much chance to play in college, because I wasn't tall enough, strong enough, and I lacked ball skills. Ouch! Again, I was devastated. My dream to play in college suddenly seemed impossible.*

*"The story could have ended there. It would have been easy to dismiss that dream and focus on something else. However, somewhere deep inside I was angry that I was letting my coach tell me it was over. It wasn't his dream, and I wasn't going to let him tell me when to give up on it. I set a goal that I was going to play college soccer, and I had a burning desire to make it happen. If anything, I was going to reach this goal just to prove him wrong.*

*"I spent the rest of that school year and summer working out on a daily basis (attendance) trying to get stronger and a little better with my ball skills. I'd go up to the school and kick against a wall, lift weights in my basement, juggle in my back yard, and run all over town instead of hanging out with my buddies (effort/perseverance). The whole time, I kept telling myself I could do it, building my confidence (attitude).*

*"To make a long story short, I went on to play four years at Western Michigan University—lettering all four years. I was never a superstar on that team, but I was very proud of my accomplishments. Despite my high school coach's opinions, I was the only member from my high school team to play four years for a Division I team.*

*"Something else worth mentioning: After my junior season in college, my coach pulled me into his office and told me he was thinking about cutting me from the team to make way for a younger player with more talent. I talked him into giving me the summer to improve. Again, I was faced with a huge challenge, and worked hard that summer to take my abilities to the next level.*

*"Not only did I make the team my senior year, but I was chosen as one of the team captains and awarded a partial scholarship by my coach.*

*"The reason I tell you this story is to help you realize that you can do it, too! You can accomplish anything you set your mind to if you're willing to work for it and not give up the first time it gets hard. Everything you need to succeed is stamped on this coin, and when I carry it in my pocket, it reminds me that I can make my best year happen over and over again."*

Hopefully, you'll be able to find a story from your own life that will capture some of the messages on the coin that you'll feel comfortable sharing with your class. I believe it's important that the students see this as something you believe in as well, because you will be their #1 coach/cheerleader at school to help them believe in this for themselves. I model how I'm using the coin to help remind me of the things I need to do to make this my best year ever.

## PART FOUR—THE COIN PROPOSITION

After everyone has held the coin and I finish discussing it, I tell them I have a proposition for them.

*"Did everyone get to hold the coin? You can see how important this is to me. How many of you would like to have a coin like this to help remind you of what you need to do to have your best year ever?"* (Hands shoot up!)

*"I'll tell you what I'll do. I'll give you twenty-four hours to think about all this. You can even go home and talk it over with your folks.*

*"If, by tomorrow, you still feel like you want to commit to having your best year ever—or one of your best years ever—and you can promise yourself—and me—that this year you'll consistently work on the three words on the back of the coin—attendance, attitude, and effort—to help yourself have your best year ever, I'll give each of you your own coin tomorrow. Does that sound like something you'd be interested in?"*

I'm pretty confident you'll get a unanimous and enthusiastic "YES!"

*"If you decide you want a Best Year Ever! coin, you have to show up tomorrow ready to commit to having your best year ever—or one of your best years ever. If you decide you don't want to do this, that's okay too—no pressure. However, if you do decide to do this, I expect you to keep your word and stay committed to this all year long.*

*"You'll also be expected to take good care of your coin. They're not cheap, as you could probably tell just by holding one. I don't mind giving you one, because I believe it's a good investment if it can help us all stay focused on what we need to do to have our best year ever. However, if you lose the coin, I can't afford to give you another one for free. So, it's important that you take good care of the coin when you get it.*

*"I want you to bring the coin to school with you each day so you can pull it out and use it when you need it to remind yourself to keep a good attitude, to give more effort, or to not give up when things get hard.*

*"On occasion, I'll randomly ask someone in the room if they have their coin. If they can show it to me, they'll earn*

the class ten extra minutes of recess or some other small
treat. I'll do things like that throughout the year as morale
builders.

"Therefore, you can see why it will be important to keep
the coin safe and have it here at school each day. You'll need
to find a safe place to keep your coin at school. Some possible
places may include your locker, trapper keeper or pocket.
You may not want to keep it in your pocket if things tend to
fall out of your pocket during recess. You've got to figure
out what will work best for you.

"I only use my coin at school. To be sure that I don't
forget it, I put it in my backpack each night before I go home.
I never leave for work without my backpack, so I know my
coin will always come to school with me each day. The first
thing I do each morning at work is take my coin out and put
it into my pants pocket. That way I have it each day and can
use it to help remind me of what I'm working on this year.

"There are two final things I want to say about the coin.
The first is that the coin is not a lucky coin. However, I do
believe you can make your luck happen by adopting, and
following, every day, the principles and ideas on this coin.

"Finally, at the end of the year, I hope the coin will make a
good keepsake to help remind you of your best year ever, and
that it reminds you that every year can be your best year
ever—if you decide to **make** it happen!

"You may have noticed that nowhere on the coin did I put
a year—like 2006—nor my name. I did that for a reason. I
hope that this coin will be useful to you longer than this
year. I didn't want you to think the year on the coin only
meant that year was your chance to have your best year
ever. Again, every year can be your best year ever.

"Also, I don't want you to think that in order to have
your best year ever you need certain teachers, bosses or

*anyone else. This year, I want you to realize that you have*
*the power to control what kind of year you want to have.*
*You are the one who can make your best year ever happen."*

The idea for waiting a day to give the coin to the students is to avoid it getting lost in the mountain of papers and forms that kids usually need to take home that first day. Also, having the kids wait twenty-four hours helps build their anticipation for getting one. I want to make sure that the first night the coin goes home, it gets center stage.

## PART FIVE—TELL THEM YOU CARE

Very early in my career, I worked next to a guy who never seemed to smile, seemed kind of gruff, and always spoke in a deep, serious tone of voice. At first I was very intimidated by him and was convinced we had nothing in common—thank goodness! However, he taught me two very valuable lessons that have helped me to grow as a teacher.

The first lesson this veteran teacher taught me was to never judge a book by its cover. He turned out to be a great person once I got to know him. He was funny, warm and very dedicated to his students. He was hugely popular with his students—especially his old students who would come back to visit him well past their college years. He was teaching his former students' kids!

Before he retired, he let me in on the secret to his success. He told me that most teachers never take the time to tell their students that they care about them. Therefore, the kids don't always know it. I still think that's the best teaching advice I've ever received.

Now, I start every year by telling my students I care about them.

*"I want to tell you something that I don't remember ever*
*hearing one of my teachers saying to me—especially at the*

*start of the year. I care about each one of you. As your teacher, I will be your biggest fan. I'll be rooting for each of you to be successful.*

*"I know you're probably thinking to yourself, 'How can this guy care about me? He barely knows me!' You're right; I don't know you yet, but I do know that you're my students, and I want you to have your best year ever. I'll spend the rest of this year showing you with my words and actions that I care about you.*

*"If you think about it, there are some good reasons why I should care about you and your success in my classroom this year. My success as a teacher is based on your success in my class. If you walk out of here at the end of the year saying, 'Wow! I had a great year. I was challenged a lot this year, grew a lot as a student, and I had a good time!' then I've done my job well and that makes me feel great.*

*"Believe it or not, the more good days you have in here means the more good days I have. Most teachers don't go home and celebrate after you have a bad day. 'Yes, I nailed Jimmy today seven times. I even got him to cry! Ha! Ha! Load up the car, Honey, I'm taking you guys out to dinner to celebrate!' Actually, just the opposite happens. After a bad day, most teachers go home with a bad headache and a sick feeling in their gut that they didn't do a good job.*

*"Think about it, I don't get paid any more or less based on your performance in here. I get the same amount of money if you pass or fail. Therefore, this can't be about money. I don't get bonuses or promotions if you do well. So why do I care about you and want you to have your* **best year ever?**

*"Pride! Knowing I'm doing my job well is my reward and incentive to help you succeed. If you're growing as a person and student this year and you feel you're having one of your*

best years ever, then I feel effective as a teacher, which makes me feel great. So, I do care about you this year, and want you to do well.

"I value my reputation as a good teacher. That's my bonus or promotion. I've worked hard to earn the reputation that makes a lot of kids want to be in here—and has their parents requesting that they be placed in here. I work just as hard to keep that reputation and build upon it. The way I do that is to strive for my best year ever each year while helping you to make this your best year ever.

"I want you to remember that I care about you, especially on those days when it seems I'm pushing you to make the right choices and to give more effort. If you think about it, it would be easier for me to look the other way and ignore certain things you shouldn't be doing than to work with you to do the right things. If I didn't care, I'd ignore the things that make my job harder and give me headaches.

"It's important that you know that even after this year is over, I won't stop caring about you. I still have old students, who are now in college, stopping in to let me know they still care about me. You'll notice that I still talk with a lot of my old students in the hallway. That's because I still care about them. You're my team now, and you will always be important to me because we will share something very special together—we'll share one of our best years ever together—and work together to make it happen.

"That's what I hope happens to us this year. We'll work hard to make our best year ever happen. Then we'll always have fond memories of what we did. So just remember—I have a lot of reasons why I care about you and why I want you to do well this year."

## PART SIX—NEW BEGINNINGS

Another important message to get out early the first day of school is to let your students know that this is a new school year—a fresh start. I let them know that I've made a point of learning as little about them as I could from previous records, past teachers or parents.

I write a quote on the board and ask the kids to look at it while I read it to them. The quote is: **"Your past doesn't equal your future."** I tell them that this is a new beginning. Their past is their business, and today marks the beginning of our working relationship and getting to know each other.

I remind them that if they've had great years in the past, that can continue this year as well. If they've struggled in the past, this is their chance to start today to redefine themselves. They have the power and control to start fresh and create their reputation any way they want.

I also reinforce to students, who had brothers/sisters in my room before, that I will give them the chance to define who *they* are. I won't compare them to their brothers or sisters because I hated it when my teachers did that to me—especially because we were nothing alike.

This is another reinforcement of the fact that this is a new, fresh start, and they have the opportunity to make this their best year ever. They can **make it happen** by doing the following:

1.     **Attendance** (show up).

2.     Have a good **attitude**.

3.     Give **effort** (try).

   **NOTE:** I don't want to learn anything about my students before we meet unless there's a medical concern. I start the year truly believing that no matter what their past has been, they'll have a great year in my room.

I really pride myself for allowing my students to define themselves without my comparing them to their brothers or sisters. However, I will occasionally make the mistake of calling them by their sibling's name. This doesn't help convince them that I'm not making comparisons.

I had one student who looked exactly like his brother, who'd been in my room the year before. These students were nothing alike except for their physical appearance. I couldn't stop calling him by his brother's name, which I knew was bugging him. I solved this problem by making a deal with him in front of the class. I told him every time I called him by his brother's name that I would owe him a "Fireball." I keep treats in the room for special occasions. After about seven Fireballs and a lot of fun, I was able to break the habit.

# Chapter Eight

# DAY TWO:  GETTING THEIR COMMITMENT

## COIN = COMMITMENT

At the start of their second day, I bring the coin out again and remind them that at the end of the day, they will have a chance to get one for themselves. To get one they must decide that they are going to make a commitment to themselves and to me to work on having their best year ever by focusing on their attendance, attitude and effort.

I wait to give it to them at the end of the day to let their anticipation grow. I believe their excitement of finally getting it will cause them to rush home and show their folks.  I pull out a bag of coins and give each student a coin if they are able to look me in the eye and say they are committed to making this their best year ever.

Again, I remind them that they need to take care of their coin and bring it to school with them each day.

Finally, I remind them that they will be getting an important letter from me, explaining what all this is about. They need to show the letter and coin to their parents.

## THE BROCHURE

As I mentioned earlier, my goal in the first couple of days of school is to generate a lot of excitement in my new group and, hopefully, in their parents. Like getting a rocket off the launch pad, it takes a huge blast-off to get that rocket soaring into outer space. I want my first couple of days to be like a huge blast-off, full of anticipation and excitement.

What I want to have happen at the end of the first day of school is for my students to run home and tell their parents something about having their best year ever, and how they're going to get a coin tomorrow if they show up and make a commitment to have good attendance, a positive attitude and to give good effort.

I really don't care *what* they say as much as *how* they say it. I want their parents to hear the excitement in their voices.

Then I want to see them go running home again at the end of the second day with a coin in their hand anxious to show it off. I want the parents to be curious and excited about the positive talk coming home with their kids—ready to hear more about what this *Best Year Ever!* approach is all about.

Now the parents will be ready for my brochure. It will explain in a little more detail—and in my own words—what this is all about. This past year I gave the coins to my students on Friday and mailed the brochures during my lunch period to get them to my students' home by Saturday. I addressed the envelopes to my students and told them on Friday I was sending them important information about the coin over the weekend, and that I wanted them to look for it and share it with their folks.

Mailing it seemed a better way to go then just sending it home with the kids. I couldn't be sure the brochures would make it home, and if they did get home, what shape they'd be in when (and if) they got to their parents. I sent them by mail hoping to make the information inside seem more important and special. By sending them to my students, I was pretty sure my envelope wouldn't get lost in the pile. What kid do you know who doesn't get excited about receiving mail?

Even though I addressed the brochure to my students, it's really intended for the parents. I want them to get a feel for how I began the year for their child and what I hope to accomplish with their child this school year. I want the parents to be clear on how I intend to use the coin, and to make it clear that this is not a mandatory part of my class. Also, I've included on the brochure a section called "A Note to Parents." This part of the brochure is aimed at giving the parents a better understanding of my teaching philosophy and my goals for the year. Finally, I want them to get a sense that this will be an extraordinary year for all involved.

I must admit that I was a little nervous sending out the brochure at first. I felt like Babe Ruth stepping up to the plate and pointing my bat toward the center-field bleachers as if to say to the world, "Watch this! I'm going to knock this next one out of here!" That's a pretty bold statement.

I mean . . . think about what I've done in two days. I've guaranteed the kids that I can give them their best year ever and put it into writing for their parents to keep like a contract. What am I doing? I'm confident in my teaching ability and feel secure knowing I usually get out of anything what I put into it, but this seems a bit extreme! Like the Babe, I'm calling my shot!

Actually, I'm turning up the pressure a little, forcing myself to commit to what I say I'm going to do. I just raised the stakes to be the best I can be this year, which will help me to have my best year ever. The fear of failure is a pretty strong motivator. I would much rather put forth a little more effort to succeed than have to face the embarrassment I'd feel if I failed to accomplish what I promised to do.

I want my students and parents to be so satisfied with their child's experience this year that they pass this brochure on to other parents who are trying to decide who would be best for their child. Let's face it—parents talk. If this can help put me in a positive light in the community, that's great! Therefore, I view this brochure as a good advertisement for who I am as a teacher. I'd better look at it that way, because I wrote it!

So, when you write your own brochure or letter, make sure it says the things that will best represent you (and your teaching style) and what you plan to accomplish during the year—*and make sure you can do it!*

The last thing I want to talk about concerning the brochure is that it provides a good starting point between student, parents and teacher. It tells everyone the goal for the year and what's needed to make it happen. I can use the terms attendance, attitude and effort whenever I'm trying to report the student's progress, with confidence that we all understand what I mean.

I use the brochure at the first parent/teacher/student conference. I set the brochure on the table, open it up, and ask the student to give an honest assessment of how they think they're doing in all three areas (attendance, attitude, effort). Then I tell them what I'm seeing, using examples of their work to help make my case. It also gives the parents a better understanding of how important I consider those three words in relation to their child's growth.

I've included the main parts of the brochure I use. Feel free to use whatever you want from it. However, I encourage you to have it written with *your own* voice coming through loud and clear. It may take a little time to write that first brochure or letter just the way you want it, but if you keep it on your computer, you can make quick changes and updates for years to come.

## Sample Brochure

This is the key information I include in my brochure. You can format this information into your own brochure or letter. Again, take what I have and alter it so that it best fits your needs. Be sure that *your* voice comes through very clearly.

---

# Welcome To Your Best Year Ever!

Imagine someone coming up to you offering you a chance to have your best school year ever. A year that you'll never forget. A year that at its end you would look back and say, "Wow! What a year!"

Well, today is your lucky day because I'm that someone. I'm offering you a chance for your best year ever.

I'm confident that I have the ability to give you one of your best school years ever. I can give you a year that will challenge and excite you and a year full of opportunities for growth.

The best part of this deal is that we'll be working together to provide and sharpen the tools you need for future best years ever!

## What's The Catch?

I can guarantee you one of your best years ever if you commit to doing all three things consistently all year long. They are the following:

- ➢ **Attendance**
- ➢ **Attitude**
- ➢ **Effort**

## ATTENDANCE
### Show Up
### Come To Class

Come to class on a regular basis so you don't fall behind or feel out of sync with the rest of the class. Challenge yourself to break your own personal record for least number of absences in one year.

## ATTITUDE
### Positive Attitude
### Belief In Self

Walk into class each day expecting something good to happen— looking for things to become excited about. Believe you can achieve whatever you set your mind to accomplish. Work with others to help them and let them help you solve problems that get in your way.

## EFFORT
### Try
### Don't Give Up

Don't worry about making mistakes. I believe that making mistakes is necessary for learning to take place. Thomas Edison made over 10,000 mistakes before he invented the light bulb. Keep trying and don't give up because you may only be one mistake away from success.

## THE COIN

Everyone in class will receive this coin to act as a *reminder* of the three things it takes to have a great year, and that *you* have the power to make it happen.

The coin is not a lucky coin. However, I do believe you can help make your *own* luck happen by choosing to follow the principles and ideas on this coin every day.

We'll find a safe place to keep the coin in the classroom. When needed, you can pull the coin out as a reminder to keep a positive attitude, give more effort and not give up.

The lit light bulb on the front of the coin represents the perseverance Thomas Edison showed when he tried over 10,000 times to invent the light bulb before succeeding. That same perseverance can be used to conquer any math problem, or any other problem you come across during the year.

I'll use the coin to help build team unity and morale. For example, on occasion I'll randomly ask to see someone's coin. If they can produce it, they'll earn the class a small treat, like five extra minutes of recess.

At the end of the year, I hope the coin will make a good keepsake to remind you of your best year ever!

## A NOTE TO PARENTS

Welcome to what I hope turns out to be a very special year for your child. I'm excited to have another school year under way. It's fun for me to receive a new group each year and get to know and work with them to create a successful team.

I'm sure by now you're wondering what all this *Best Year Ever!* talk is all about. Let me start by saying that I'm not trying to compete with or take away from any of your child's past teachers or experiences in school. I believe there can never be too many good teachers and experiences for your child!

I've been teaching over twenty years now, and each year I start off with the same goal. I try to make each upcoming year my best year yet! At the end of the year, I want to be able to look back and see that I challenged myself by trying new things, found more effective ways to reach my students' needs, provided a safe, positive learning environment and had fun getting to know and working with my group.

I told your child on the first day that I could guarantee that they would have one of their best years ever in school this year if they made a commitment to learn and master three words I presented to them: *Attendance, Attitude* and *Effort.*

I truly believe that this is an attainable goal for them based on the success I've had using this approach with past groups. I believe in setting high goals that will be exciting to work toward, and then working hard to make them a reality.

Although I feel this is an attainable goal, it will take the cooperation and support of us working together to make this year a success for your child. As I told the class this week, my success as a teacher is based on their success. I'm going to be their number one fan this year, and do whatever I can to help them have a fantastic year.

The coin your child received will be used to help build team unity and morale while, hopefully, serving as a powerful reminder that they can make their goals a reality.

The expense of the coins came out of my pocket. I feel it is a good investment if the coins play a positive role in your child's school year. However, I can't afford to replace lost coins, so I will encourage the kids to take good care of them. I can replace coins for $2.00, which covers the cost of each coin. It is *not* mandatory that your child has a coin. This is intended to be a fun motivation, and I'll work to keep it that way!

**Bill Cecil (2006-2007)**

Chapter Nine

# CREATING A CARING COMMUNITY

After we plant the seeds of success in each child's mind during the first two days of school, *we*, then, must create a caring community that will act as a healthy "garden" in which those seeds can grow and thrive throughout the school year.

Therefore, during the first few weeks of school your main goal is to create an environment where diverse individuals can come together and work as a team to accomplish common and individual goals while striving for their own personal best. The environment should enable everyone to understand their role on the team and to be aware of how their contribution to the team is essential to reach its goals.

As the leader of your team, you must create an environment where each member of the team feels respected and valued. Each member of the team needs to feel a responsibility to help others on the team be successful, because they understand that the team is only as strong as its weakest link.

As I mentioned earlier, by creating a winning team in your classroom, you'll give your students a chance to experience something many people crave but usually only get to experience indirectly. You'll also provide your students with a very focused and caring environment where each student can work to develop successful strategies for the future while, hopefully, having one of their best years ever.

Like other winning teams, don't be surprised if you start to have fans. Students, parents, and administrators will undoubtedly hear about the success stories coming out of your room, and will want to be a part of it. Like other winning teams, your students will stand out as a group that is focused and works well together.

This may sound like a pretty tall order to fill, but you already have the beginnings of your recipe for success. Go back and reread the four strategies covered in *Setting the Table for Success* that are covered in *Section One* of this book. As you start to implement these powerful strategies in your classroom, continue to read on to get the second part of the success formula that will help you build your own winning team.

## CREATING A FORMULA FOR SUCCESS

As I work to set the table and start to serve the meal in my classroom, these are the five areas on which I focus each day to help keep the team strong and focused. These five areas, which overlap in many cases, are essential to keep the team together. I spend the first month really trying to build a sense of team in our classroom. Once the team is developed, it takes very little time and energy to keep it going. The kids will eventually share in the responsibility for keeping the team united and working together to reach our goals.

The areas, which make up the acronym, **TEAMS**, are:

**T**arget Talk

**E**nvironment

**A**ll Involved

**M**odel Management

**S**ervice

These are the five areas I consistently focus on to help keep my team strong and things running smoothly in my classroom.

They don't take a lot of time away from your day once they're in place. I want to discuss each one carefully and explain what it looks like and sounds like in my classroom.

## T= TARGET TALK

Basically, target talk is talking about the things you want the kids to think about. Going back to the garden analogy, if I didn't take the time to weed the garden, the weeds would eventually take over and strangle the plants.

I have no idea what my students are always thinking. I can't sit around hoping they're thinking about the things that will help them have their best year ever, or help them to be better teammates. I have to help pluck out negative thinking and fertilize the healthy plants (thoughts) so they'll grow.

I once read a quote that said basically, *"You become what you think you are."*

I interpret that to mean that what you focus your thoughts and energy on, you eventually become. I want the kids to focus on doing and thinking certain things in the classroom on a regular basis, so I purposely work it into whatever we're talking about or learning about that day.

Let me give you three examples of how I do this.

**First example** is that I want to talk about the words "attendance," "attitude" and "effort" throughout the day because it ties into the kids working toward their best year ever. Instead of my standing in front of the class and drilling them with how important it is that they continue to work on these three words, I want to find a way to work it into my day—like hitting a target.

At the start of the afternoon, I read aloud to the kids from a book I choose (target book) about a boy who has never done well in school but ends up having his best year ever. The book is Louis Sachar's *There's a Boy in the Girls' Bathroom.*

As I read, I may find specific examples where the struggling little boy, Bradley, is unhappy about his situation, and I ask my students to tell me what word on the back of their *Best Year Ever!* coin he is not using in his life.

This can lead to a great mini-discussion the kids are controlling rather than a lecture from me. It carries more weight because it's coming from them, and they're connecting it to something we're learning about or doing. It helps to make those three words more important and real to them because they can see how it applies to something we're studying or how it applies to Bradley's life.

**Second example** is that every two to three weeks, I choose a new *social skill* (cooperative learning) to focus on. During that time, I'll try to target-talk that skill as much as I can to really focus on it, and then I'll use it occasionally afterward to keep it alive in the room.

Let's say the skill I'm focusing on during a time period is *initiative*. Anytime I see someone in the room taking initiative, I will say something like, "I just saw Nancy take initiative by picking up Bernard's paper for him."

When I do that enough times, pretty soon they'll start using the target talk themselves. That's when you know your target talk is working. If they're using the words, they're probably modeling them as well—or seeing them being modeled by others.

Often, I will overuse target talk with a specific word I feel they need to be working on to the point that they find it funny, and we can joke about it. Again, they'll start using the targeted word to get me to laugh, but they also focus on that word or idea until it starts to be modeled more consistently in class.

**NOTE:** This is a very positive way to get kids to think about the behaviors you want them to be thinking about without sounding like you're preaching to them.

**Example Three** is that each morning, the very first thing I say to the group is, "Good morning, everyone, and welcome to day 78 of your *Best Year Ever!* I'm glad to see that you're still working to make it happen!"

This is a positive way to start each day by replanting that very powerful thought in each of their minds: That this is a goal from day one. It takes less than one minute out of my busy day.

I know they'll focus on this, because I also keep the number of what day we're on written on the blackboard. If I forget to change that number before they come in, I'll hear about it. This shows that they are paying attention to this, so to show respect I try not to forget.

### What Should You Target-Talk About?

Basically, I target-talk about any and every behavior I want the kids to work on in the classroom. It's like I'm giving little subliminal reminders throughout the day to do the things that will help us stay focused and united.

I may be going over a group assignment and getting them ready to work on their own. As I'm giving the directions about how to do the actual assignment, I also throw in a couple reminders to work together as a team, be willing to look for a positive solution to any problem that may arise, and to give this their best effort while keeping the noise level down.

Again, this takes little time, but it reminds the students that teamwork is important in our room. It reminds them not to come running up to me to solve all their little problems, and it pushes them to give this assignment their best effort. Also, it reminds them I'll be looking for that, and it's a reminder that I want them to monitor their own noise level as they work.

Target talk is a way to constantly let your expectations for the class be known before a problem occurs. The most common areas that I try to target-talk during the day are:

**Working to Have *Your* Best Year Ever!**

**You Have the Power to Make Your Goals Happen**

**Attendance/Attitude/Effort**

**Examples of Perseverance**

**Reminders to Challenge Self**

**We're a Team**

**Team Work**

**Team Pride**

**Life Skills/Social Skills**

**Conflict Resolution Strategies**

**Responsibility to Help Others Follow Our Rules**

Again, I make a conscious effort to continually look for places during our day to target-talk about the things I believe will keep our team running like a fine-tuned machine instead of waiting for a problem to arise and then try to deal with it. *This is a proactive approach instead of a reactive one.*

The more I practice using target talk, the more natural my teaching becomes. People working in my room with me often comment about how many times I throw out little positive reminders or make connections to what we're learning, and how it seems to make a positive difference in my room. What I really enjoy is when the kids make a connection to something we're reading or learning about before I do, or I hear them using target talk with each other in a positive way.

## E = ENVIRONMENT

Did you ever walk into another teacher's room and immediately get a sense that they have a nice room? It feels good! You know what I mean? In less than twenty seconds, you get a feeling that this would be a nice place to be everyday.

Or have you ever walked into a room and immediately gotten a different feeling? It isn't welcoming or comfortable. Something just doesn't feel right, and it's a room you're anxious to get out of as soon as you can.

A few years ago, I had the opportunity to help out in the office for a couple of days when my principal was at a conference. I was helping with some of the assistant principal's jobs while she covered more of the principal's duties.

I spent a lot of time walking around the school, going in and out of classrooms, delivering messages and pulling out students who had some kind of problem earlier in the day to work with them.

I was amazed at the different feelings I got as I walked into the different rooms. In some rooms, I felt immediately welcomed like a guest, and in some I felt like an unwanted trespasser. Some rooms felt warm and inviting, while others felt chaotic, and some were sterile and cold.

Because of that experience, I went back and took a closer look at what kind of learning environment I'd created for my kids to work in, and what kinds of messages it was giving to others. Since that time, I'm very deliberate about how I set up my room to make sure it matches what I'm trying to do.

I believe the atmosphere of the room and the room's environment play a major part in the performance and feelings of those working in it. I always felt excited to play on a freshly cut, well-lined soccer field. It made me feel more professional, and that's how I wanted to perform.

The same is true when I see a theatre production. The first thing I can't help but focus on is the set. If it looks good, it makes me want to jump up on stage and perform. I'm already enjoying the show, even before it begins. If the set looks thrown together, it's a distraction for me even if the acting and the story are interesting. Therefore, I want my room to motivate my students to want to come in each day ready to give it their best. These are some of the main things I try to concentrate on when I set up my room for success.

## Be Professional Looking

I tell my students that this is our office; not our home. I have no idea how messy or neat they are in their homes, so I tell them we'll keep it looking like a place of business. Most businesses keep their work environment very clean.

We have a rule that we don't leave anything out on our desks when we leave the room, and our chairs are pushed in and the floor is clean. Because we have lockers, I don't let kids keep their jackets draped over the backs of their chairs, nor do I let them keep their backpacks on the floor next to them.

At the end of the day, I do not dismiss the kids until their chairs are up, and the floor is swept. I remind them that it's not the custodian's job to pick up after us, but rather to keep the building clean and operating. I want them to take ownership in keeping our room nice looking—even after the end of the day.

NOTE: It takes my students, working together, less than five minutes to get all the chairs up and the floor swept. I had no idea how much this really meant to my custodial staff, until one day, when they walked in during my class and presented my students with an award for having the cleanest room in the school. They later told me that most teachers expect them to put up the chairs or move them around themselves before mopping. That's a lot of added time to do something that would take little time for each class to do.

### Positive Messages

I place some of my favorite quotes around the room; things I want the children to think about. I read and explain each quote in detail during the first few days of school, and use them throughout the year whenever I can make a connection to what we are doing or talking about.

Sign under clock: **"Happiness Is A Choice."**

**Explanation:** It's a reminder to the child who is just sitting staring at the clock that it's *time* for an attitude check. Also, it's a reminder that you control how you feel—and you can *choose* to be happy.

> **NOTE:** I tell the kids I don't expect anyone to be happy all the time, but that it's important for them to realize it's their choice to feel whatever they choose to feel in any situation. Don't sit in class waiting for someone else to make them happy or interested, find something to get excited about. They have the power to do it themselves.

Sign on News/Current Events Bulletin Board: **"The Way You Choose To See The World Creates The World You See."**

**Explanation:** YOU SEE WHAT YOU FOCUS ON! If you focus on all the bad in the world, you'll see the world as a bad and scary place. If you focus on a lot of the good in the world, you'll see the world as a good place.

> **Exercise:** Have the kids focus on a certain color in the room and ask them to name everything they see that is that color in their room. They'll start to notice that color all over the place. Next, ask them to focus on another color—let's say yellow—and then have them close their

eyes and name everything in the room that's red. It will be hard for them to name any because they weren't focusing on that color.

Tell the children that the same is true with what they decide to focus on in their life and world. If all one looks for is bad, they will only see bad. And the same is true if one looks for good. They will be in the habit of seeing mostly good in their life/world.

NOTE: I tell the kids that it's our responsibility this year to bring in news articles that aren't just reporting bad news. It will be important to dig a little and find good news so we can show a more realistic view of our world; not the world the papers are creating to help sell more papers.

Sign in front (center) of room: **"You Are as Smart as You Choose to Be."**

**Explanation:** You can do whatever you choose to do in life if you believe you can do it. If you tell yourself you "can't," your brain will search for a way to prove you're right. There is nothing I can do for you if you believe you can't.

If you say you "can" or "will," your brain will search for clues to prove you right.

Asking quality questions will lead to success! Be aware of how you ask and word your questions because it will determine what you focus on. Instead of asking, "Why can't I do this?" say, "What can I do to learn this?"

Sign over water fountain by our door: **"Make It Happen!"**

**Explanation:** Don't just wish it—Make It Happen! You have the power to make it happen—whatever "it" is—especially when you approach it (school) with a positive attitude.

**NOTE:** Remind kids that the coin's "Make It Happen!" slogan applies to everything we've talked about. You *can* choose to be happy. You *can* choose to see the world as a world of good and opportunity. You *can* create the world you want to see. You *can* be as smart as you choose to be. You *can* have a good attendance record. You *can* give effort consistently.

You *can* make mistakes and grow from them. You *can* set and achieve goals this year. You *can* focus on what you want to become or do. You *can* tackle your "cannots." You *can* have your **Best Year Ever!** You *can* **Make It Happen!**

**Idea:** Make that into an overhead and put it up every so often and say it as a class pledge.

### Personal Touch

By adding some personal touches around the room, not only will your room look and sound professional, it will feel comfortable. Little pieces of my life or personality are splashed around the room to give people a better idea of who I am.

I have family pictures on my desk and plastered on one file cabinet. I have gifts from former students positioned around the room. The Three Stooges seem to be the theme of many of my gifts. I have Three Stooges coffee mugs holding pencils, pens and name sticks. I have a Three Stooges poster in one corner of the room and a few Three Stooges figurines by my telephone.

I have no idea how I got labeled as a Three Stooges guy, but I don't mind. The kids have a lot of fun with it, and it gives them something other than just school-related topics to talk to me about. Students will often bring school pictures of themselves to share with me. I make sure to put them up in the room so that the room becomes more personal to them, too.

**Idea:** An activity I do at the start of every school year is ask the kids to cut out magazine pictures of things they identify with in some way. After they have enough pictures to cover a piece of drawing paper, I ask them to arrange their collage and glue it down. Once everyone has completed a collage, I put all the collages on a wall right outside our room as one huge collage. I stick a sign in the middle of if that says, "IDENTIFY OUR IDENTITIES!"

I tell the kids that our collage represents our team, because it's made up of a bunch of diverse individuals coming together to get the job done. The kids love to have their parents and friends try to guess which one represents them. I usually leave it up until after our open house event.

It doesn't take much, but a little personal touch can go a long way toward making your room a more inviting, friendly place to work.

### A Team Room

How many classrooms have you walked into and seen the team's goals posted on big chart paper on the wall for all to see? My guess is, not too many! The first thing you'll most likely see when you walk into my classroom is a huge piece of yellow chart paper that has our team's goals listed on it.

I position our team's goals on the wall across from the door to serve as a reminder to each of us that we're on a team and we're working together to reach our goals by the end of the year. The kids have worked together to set our goals; therefore they're more committed to them.

I will target-talk our goals often during the year, walking over to our goals sheet or asking the children to silently read them or have someone read them to the class. I don't let the kids forget that the goals are there.

The work tables are arranged so that students can work in small groups when needed. Four desks pushed together, facing each other, works great to help build smaller teams/communities within the larger group.

I make it clear to the team early on the first day of school that this is not "my room," but "our room." I tell them that I don't lock things up and won't lock things up unless I'm given a reason to. I want people to not only feel that they're safe in this room, but also that their things will be safe as well. Again, this is a topic for target talk early and often throughout the year.

I tell them that I'm more than willing to share my things with them as long as they ask first. I also remind them that I'll do the same for them. I will not borrow their things without first getting permission. We set up an agreement the very first day that says we will not get into each other's desks without permission.

Other than each other's desks, I really don't have too many "no zones" in my classroom. I want them to feel it's their room as much as mine.

## Safe

In the front of the room, I post our rules that we worked together to develop ourselves. We work hard the first few weeks to learn and master our rules. I tell my students that I post the rules in the front of the room, because they're the most important thing to help make our room a safe, positive learning environment.

I make it clear that I *will not tolerate* anyone on our team bullying another person on our team—or other teams—with words or actions. I explain that this includes name calling, eye rolling and ignoring teammates. I tell them this is the one thing that I'll become angry about this year, both because it's wrong to treat anyone that way, and because it will prevent us from becoming a team that others in the building will recognize as a special group. I tell them that up front so it does not become an issue later.

I have a feeling that a lot of teachers expect kids to know that, but if you don't make it clear to them at the start of the year, it could become a constant thorn in your side.

I tell them my number one goal is to keep them safe this year, and I need their help to get that done. They usually respond very well to this statement.

*Fun*

A common complaint I hear from teachers is that kids don't want to work; they just want to have fun—and a common complaint from kids is that school is boring.

Someone taped an article on our teachers' lounge door a year ago about how hard it is for teachers to compete with TV and video games. It was describing all the ways children are different today and why they're hard to teach. The person writing the article was basically saying that it's not a teacher's job to make school fun.

I couldn't disagree more. I tend to side more with *Highlights* magazine. Their mission statement is "Fun with a Purpose." That's a cool mission statement. That's how I'd like to describe my life—work included.

I believe that not everything we do in school is fun or designed to be fun. However, I think one can still go about it with a fun attitude. I tend to work harder when I'm having fun and enjoying what I'm doing. I think of it as the gas that fills my tank.

I use humor in my classroom like a good chef uses seasoning. If you use the right amount at the right time, it can really spice up the meal/lesson. I tell my kids that I'll use humor as much as they show me they can handle it. If they get too silly or won't focus on the task, then I pull back. However, if they can use it to work harder longer, I keep it going.

I tell the kids that humor is never funny at the expense of others, and it's important that we never go for a cheap laugh. I model very carefully the type of humor I believe is appropriate for the team.

I tell my students I'm always looking for better/more exciting ways to do my job, because then, I'm not bored. That's how I gauge things in my room. I get bored if I'm doing too much of the same things, and I know that if I'm bored, the kids must be bored.

Granted—not everything can be fun or made exciting, but I believe the kids are more willing to work through those assignments knowing that something more interesting or fun will be coming down the pike soon enough. I think they appreciate the fact that I'm working hard to find ways to make their learning experience more fun—which is another way I show them I care—and therefore they work harder for me.

Last, what great modeling it is to show the kids that, as an adult in the workplace, you can really enjoy yourself while working hard to get the job done.

## A = ALL INVOLVED

In my classroom, I stay away from the "us vs. them" mentality. The words "we" and "our" are very important on my team. I want my class to really understand that "we" are in this together. However, we all have specific roles to play, and even though "our" roles may be different, we all need each other to reach our team goals.

### Just Don't Call Me "Sue"

If I'm not mistaken, there's a really great old Johnny Cash song called, *"A Boy Named Sue."* In this song, the boy named

Sue didn't mind if you called him a whole bag of names, but he'd get extremely bummed if you called him Sue.

That sort of fits calling me a teacher. I love being called a teacher, but I believe I play many other roles as well. I think my favorite role is that of a motivational speaker. When playing that role, my job is to help my students see the need for making a change or setting a goal, help them to believe they can accomplish it, and then help them take action. When I play this role well, I feel most satisfied as a teacher.

I also like to think of myself as a coach or manager, guiding my team to be able to work together in such an effective and efficient manner that it increases our winning or productivity. My biggest challenge is to lead them to a point where they're able to perform at their highest level as consistently as possible.

I also see myself as their biggest fan and cheerleader at school. I'm truly cheering for their success and cheering them on. Once the kids figure this out, they won't want to let you down.

Finally, as the year goes on, I see myself as their facilitator more than their teacher. They become more independent and take on more responsibility towards their education. My favorite quote related to my role as facilitator fits here.

**"We must view young people not as empty bottles to be filled, but as candles to be lit."**

**— Robert H. Shaffer**

In a nutshell, that's my goal as a motivational speaker, coach, manager, cheerleader, fan, facilitator, and yes—a teacher. If they come to me with a flame lit, I want to stoke that flame so that it's a torch when they leave. If they come to me without a flame, by the end of the year there will definitely be one burning brightly.

**Idea:** One way I make sure to stay involved is that I don't sit at my teacher's desk, *ever!* I sit all over the room, but never at my desk. I tell them they will never see me at my desk because, as a child, that's where most of my teachers sat. It was like their fortress to separate them from their students.

I usually sit at one of the back seats so that at times that becomes the front of the classroom. I can have certain kids near me without making it obvious. Also, I don't usually get complaints from parents about their child sitting in the back of the room, because I move around so much during the day that there really is no back of the class.

My favorite moments are when people come in looking for me and start to walk out, thinking I'm not in the room. When I let them know I'm there, they'll then say something like, "I didn't see you. You blend right in with the kids." That's the way it should be!

### The Players

Much of my early training as a teacher came from studying and taking workshops on cooperative learning. This remains a huge part of how I manage my room and the people in it.

My whole philosophy of "all involved" comes from that exposure to cooperative learning. If you're familiar with cooperative learning, a lot of what I'm about to talk about should sound familiar.

### Learning Partners

Every student in the room is responsible for helping at least one other student. I assign learning partners as soon as I get a feel for the kids and some of their strengths and needs. I always team up the leaders with the followers. By doing this, I have a bunch of little field generals out there doing a lot of my work for me.

A learning partner's main responsibility is to make sure their partner knows what they've missed when they're out of the room for whatever reason, whether absences or for student council. It's also the learning partner's job to make sure their partner stays on task during a lesson or during an independent work time, answering any questions they may have along the way.

### Expectations For Working Relationships

Usually, not only will I match up leaders with followers, but I will match up girls with boys. I try to keep buddies from years past not seated together to help avoid cliques and encourage everyone to get in the habit of working with as many new people as possible.

Before I move seats after the first day, I give a little target talk, explaining my expectations for students being able to work together in my room. I tell the kids I expect everyone to establish a good working relationship with *everyone* in the room, because they'll be working with many different people all year long. I explain that they don't have to be "friends" with everyone in the room, but that I shouldn't be able to tell who is and is not a friend when they're working together. I give them the example that I must work with everyone in my building even though not everyone in my building is my friend.

I tell them, "In this room, we all work together and are expected to get along. Who you hang out with outside of work is your choice. I don't expect you to all hold hands skipping to the malt shop together after work to get a shake. At work, I expect you to be able to work with anyone without any complaints, because that will keep everyone on the team feeling appreciated and valued."

### Team Building Exercises

During the first couple weeks of school, I use a lot of theater games and team-building exercises to help build my team. Some of these exercises will be mentioned in *Appendix 1*. I'll use this same approach whenever I move seats, which is about three or four times a year.

### Learning Teams

Learning teams are made up of the four students sitting at each table. If someone's learning partner is unable to help, there are two more people at the table who can help. I encourage my students to ask their learning partner, their learning team and, as a last resort, me if they have a question about something we're working on during a work period. I want them to become responsible for each other.

### Team Captains

Each week I choose a new "captain" in each group, who is responsible for helping make sure certain assignments get done, who gathers materials for the group and collects and turns in assignments when due. This gives everyone a chance to be the team captain for the week.

### "Rally Round" What?

There are a number of cooperative learning techniques designed to give everyone a fair chance to share and be heard. Three techniques I often use in my room are:

- ◆ "Rally Robin"
- ◆ "Round Robin"
- ◆ "Round Table"

I use these all the time, because they're quick and easy, and they get everyone involved in sharing their ideas in a very small amount of time. It beats trying to give everyone a chance to share one at a time, and it forces participation from those students who tend not to participate.

**NOTE:** Check the Bibliography for a great book called *Cooperative Learning*, by Dr. Spencer Kagan, that will give you much more detail about how to effectively use cooperative learning and these three strategies in your classroom.

### Group Challenges/Competitions/Celebrations

Finally, I design small-group projects and activities that require everyone in the group to participate. Sometimes I design games that pit the teams against each other for small treats. The rules of the game expect everyone to be prepared to answer the question or perform the task.

More often at the start of the year, I'll award a group a small treat for working the best together or coming up with the longest brain-stormed list for the topic being discussed. These are random so they have no idea when they're coming. My hope is that this continually keeps them on their toes.

## M = MODEL MANAGEMENT

There are seven things on which I focus when trying to manage my class on a daily basis. They are:

### Clear Expectations

Using target talk, I clearly define what the accepted behavior and noise level will be for each of the following situations:

♦ Structured times – in the classroom working on a lesson with me.

♦ Slightly less structured times – working on a group project in the room.

♦ Finally, little structure — playing outside for recess.

All activities fit one of these structured time periods. Therefore, I let them know that I have a few expectations for any situation.

The first one is called "Doing the Right Thing Because It's the Right Thing to Do!"

Doing the right thing because it's the right thing to do means that the students are not trying to pull an Eddie Haskel (*Leave It To Beaver*) or an Angelica (*Rugrats*). These two characters are always polite and well-mannered when an adult is around, but as soon as no adult is looking, they show their true selves and try to get away with something.

I tell the kids that I want to be able to trust that they're choosing to do the right things this year because they are the right things to do, and because they feel right.

Integrity is another topic on which I spend a great deal of time early in the year. Then, I throw that word out to them every so often during the year when the situation seems appropriate.

I tell the students, "Your integrity is like your reputation. It's one of the few things in the world no one can take from you. You can be flat broke, living on the street, and still have your integrity. However, you can give little pieces of your integrity away without even realizing it—and once it's gone, it's *much* harder to get it back."

**Example:** A student may come to me and say that something from their desk is missing, like a pencil. Instead of having some big melt-down, I'll ask the class to look for that student's pencil. I know no one in the class would be willing to give a piece of their integrity away for something I would have been glad to give them if they'd just asked. I make it clear that the pencil must be misplaced or someone picked it up by mistake, because we don't have that sort of problem in our room. Usually the pencil is "found" and returned.

Our team's reputation is also huge. I tell the kids that I want us to stand out as the best group to work with in the building. I target-talk this one almost every time before my team works with another staff member in the building or before going to an assembly.

I tell the kids that the way we walk down the hall should make us stand out as being a special group. We actually practice lining up single file and walking down the hallway. Our goal is to walk down the hall in such a way that no one has to close their door when we pass by. This becomes almost a fun challenge for the kids, and they often remind themselves of our expectations.

> **NOTE:** What teacher doesn't want their kids to walk down the hallway in a civilized manner? And yet, many teachers don't take the time to explain why that's important and how it can benefit their team. Most will say, "Line-up and don't talk!" Or they'll have no expectations, and that shows, too.

I think teachers sometimes assume too much and then become disappointed when their students don't do the right things. I believe that if one establishes clear expectations and an understanding of why they are important, the children will usually respond.

### Rules and Consequences

I have lots of expectations, but few rules—five, to be exact. I ask the kids to work with me the first day of school to help create the five rules that will help us to have a positive, safe, learning environment and give us a better chance to have our best year ever.

**NOTE:** This activity is described in detail in *Appendix 1* under *Rules Workshop*.

Once we agree on our five rules, I post them in the front of the room and discuss each one, describing what that rule should look and sound like in the room. I model each rule to clarify to everyone exactly what I'm looking for.

I have positive and negative consequences in my room for following or breaking the rules. I take time to go over the consequences to make sure they're clear to everyone. I explain that negative consequences are just as important as the positive ones, because they act as a deterrent.

**Example:** I'm known as the "Dictionary King" because I'll ask the students to look up a few words when they have a late assignment. I tell them it's like a speeding ticket. If I decided to speed on the way home from school, the ticket will cost me around $80. That's a lot of money, and that will remind me not to speed next time I'm in my car. If the officer didn't give me a ticket, what would keep me from doing it again? Therefore, I think that having consequences to fit the crime (broken rule) is fair.

I also have plenty of positive consequences to reward the kids for good behavior—like bonus recess time, team awards, team assist awards and treats.

### Respectful

Respect is important in my room. I don't want to embarrass anyone into behaving. It's not worth winning that battle only to lose the war with that child, because now, he hates me for embarrassing him.

Like the example above about the speeding ticket, I think it's fair for the police officer to give me a ticket for breaking a law I know is in place, and know the consequences if caught. However, I don't think it would be fair for that officer to jerk me out of my car and yell in my face about what kind of moron I am for everyone on the highway to see.

I feel the same way about how to discipline students. Don't embarrass them, and they'll respect you more for that. Also, I work hard to let the kids know I may not have cared for their *behavior*, but I still care for *them*.

## Fair

I try to be as fair as possible when it comes to student discipline. I never want kids to feel they're being picked on or singled out. Sometimes it's tempting when that always-perfect student slips up and forgets an assignment. Part of me wants to say don't worry about it—especially if they start to tear up—but I don't, because of the message it sends to everyone else. (Also, I don't think it's all bad for the perfect kid to slip up once in a while and see that the world did not come to a crashing end.)

Sometimes, if I get stuck between trying to figure out the fairest way to handle a situation, I'll ask the kids involved what they would do if they were me trying to make it fair for everyone. They usually are harder on themselves then I would be, but they walk away believing that was a fair way to deal with it.

## Consistent

I don't care whether it's Monday morning, two minutes left in the day on Friday afternoon, the middle of the year, or the last day of school—my expectations for the students to follow the rules don't change.

I tell the students that I'm not in the classroom to catch them doing things wrong. I want them to succeed, but I wouldn't be a very good or honest teacher if I ignored the bad things because I didn't want to deal with them or sound negative. I tell them the first day of school that I care about them, and that when I work with them to correct a poor choice or bad behavior, that's one way I show that I care. I say, "Sometimes it would be easier for me to look the other way, but I know it will not help you or the rest of the class to let those little things slide."

I make it clear to them that I get no pleasure out of getting them into trouble or calling their folks to explain the problem their child is having. However, it's not worth it to me to give up a piece of my integrity to lie to them or their folks about what I'm seeing.

### Positive/Proactive

Again, having clear expectations and using target-talk, I approach my management in a very positive way. I tell them what I want before I ask them to do something—even something as simple as lining up in the hall—and then I make sure they are doing it right and praise that behavior/choice.

I also have built-in ways for the kids to watch over each other and monitor themselves.

> **Idea:** I have the students working together to earn their recess each day. It's quite simple to earn recess. All they have to do is end the day without two checks on the board. However, if they get two checks in one day, they lose recess and write the rules during that time to refocus on what they as a team need to be doing to be successful.

I give checks when more than a few members of the team are not following directions, staying focused on our work, leaving a mess out when we leave the room, or not completing a transition within a set amount of time.

For example, I may say, "You have thirty seconds to put math away and get out your spelling folder." If time counts down and six kids are still lagging behind, I will put a check on the board and remind the group why they got the check and how, with each other's positive reminders, they could have gotten this done.

That's it! No long lecture, just a real quick reminder of what my expectations were, how they slipped up, and how they can succeed in the future.

I'll sometimes first draw a square where the checks will go to give them a warning.

What's amazing is that later during the day, all I have to do is walk over to the box as if I'm going to put a check up and the kids will quickly monitor and adjust their behavior—without my having to say a word! This works great when we have a visitor speaking in the room, and I don't feel we're giving him or her our best.

Early in the year, you have to be willing to lose a recess and put up the second check—preferably on a really nice weather day. This sends the message that you really won't hesitate to take away a recess—even on a really nice day.

It never fails that someone will say that they weren't doing anything wrong, and therefore, it's not fair they lost their recess. I tell them that I love recess too, because it lets me get outside and talk to my friends. I tell them it's similar to when I used to play soccer. In some games I may be playing great and even score a goal. But if we aren't playing well as a team and our defense lets up three goals, we still lose. I still lose the game despite my good performance.

I remind them that if only one or two people were struggling with one of our rules, I would have worked with them on that and would not have given the class the check. I give the check only when more than a few are not doing something that needs to be done. Again, I remind them to remind each other in a positive way to help each other make smart choices.

On average, I only lose three to four recesses per year—which, considering the strong impact this has in my room to help keep the kids watching out for each other, is a good investment.

### Modeling

Finally, I constantly model what I want the kids to do. Seriously, I don't just tell the kids what I want; I show them! Sometimes I'm very serious when I model what I want done, and many times I exaggerate so the kids think it's funny while getting a clear understanding of what I want from them. Try it. You will be surprised what you get out of it. (We all have a secret little "ham" in us.)

**Example:** Earlier, I used the example of the police officer giving me the ticket. I'll play out both good cop/bad cop scenarios, exaggerating their behavior. I then take them through the two different scenarios of how a teacher can discipline in these classrooms. I usually start with the bad teacher first and exaggerate their behavior with a student, and then I repeat the scene with a good teacher maintaining the student's dignity while the teacher disciplines them. In a fun way, I've made a strong point.

Also, while teaching, I model to the kids what it looks and sounds like to be an active, positive and caring teammate. When we work with others, I make sure to use plenty of "pleases" and "thank yous" and make sure I'm being an active listener and showing respect.

**Idea:** When someone comes into your room to work with your kids—like an art enhancer or D.A.R.E. officer—don't sit at your desk and grade papers. Get involved in the activity as if you were one of the students. It's a great way to show them that you value this activity as being important, and it gives you a great chance to model how they should be going about the activity.

## S = SERVICE

I try to be the Home Depot of teachers when it comes to customer service. Home Depot is one of many builders' superstores which are virtually the same—except for one very important difference. Home Depot, from the minute you walk in their doors until the staff helps you load up your car and thanks you for shopping with them, is customer service driven.

The customer-service driven staff makes it clear that you are the reason they're there, and they need you to be happy to help keep them in business. They seem to truly care about you and show that concern in how they work with you to serve your needs.

A quick story to help illustrate this point: A few years ago, I went to Home Depot to buy a new gas grill. I was so excited to get it home, I didn't take the time to secure it safely in the back of my truck. On the way home, you can imagine my surprise when my four-year-old (at the time) reported that our grill was flying out of our truck. The grill was broken beyond repair.

When I called Home Depot to tell them what had happened, and that it was my fault, they didn't hesitate to assure me they would gladly replace it free of charge.

When I went back, they helped me unload the old one, pick out a new one, and helped me secure it safely in my truck, never once making me feel like the fool I was.

It's no wonder that Home Depot continues to do well despite all its competition. Treating your customers as though they are Number One is a great formula for success.

I try to treat my students and their parents like they are my customers, and I'm working with my students to make their year in my room the best experience they can get. It doesn't mean that I lower my expectations for them or grade them soft to please their folks. It means that I try to remember—even under difficult situations—that I'm working with them to find a way to make everyone happy with the outcome. It's not "my way or the highway."

"Customer service" is the one area I believe most schools and teachers should never stop working on.

Well, there you have it. You now have a powerful game plan to use in your classroom to help every student succeed. By using this plan, and the activities covered in *Appendix 1*, you will be able to create a positive, safe and productive learning environment that will enable everyone to have their **Best Year Ever!**

# AFTERWORD

While writing this book, I often pictured myself as an impassioned coach trying to deliver a motivating pre-game locker room speech trying to help prepare you for the big game ahead. I wanted to give you a pep talk while providing you with a doable plan, so you'd feel confident and excited as you charge onto the playing field of this great profession—your classroom.

I hope this book will motivate you to become one of the many leaders in education we so badly need right now. I hope that somewhere within these pages you started to get a clear vision of where you want to lead your team.

I'm confident I've provided you with a doable plan that you can use to create your own winning teams. I believe that by taking the needed time and using the ideas and strategies I shared in *Setting the Table for Success* and *Best Year Ever!—A Year Long Theme That Focuses on Team*, you have all the tools you need to get this done, tools that took me years to discover or create on my own.

Like a coach, I can have a great game plan on paper and a bunch of plays that I think will help you win. I can talk until I'm blue in the face to get you fired up to play; but I can't win the game for you. When the game starts, it will take *you*, working the plan, to get the job done.

I will judge the success of this book by how well it helps you succeed in your classroom.

There are two ways I'll be able to tell how you're doing. First, I'll keep my eye on the statistics that report the percent of novice teachers leaving teaching within five years. My hope is that number will drop dramatically as more people read and use my book.

Second, I hope many of you will take the time to contact me and let me know how you're doing, first hand. Go to my website (www.BestYearEver.net) or email me (BillCecil@BestYearEver.net). Please feel free to contact me at any time with questions or concerns you have or to just let me know how well you're doing. Think of me as an on-line mentor who's always available for you to lean on, confide in, and celebrate with.

Last, I'm going to ask you to help me help others in need. If, after reading and using this book you feel it's helped you become more successful in leading and managing your team, please share it with as many other teachers or teachers in training as possible. Please let them know how much this book has helped you and point them to my website so they can order their own copy.

Let me be one of the first to welcome you to this noble profession and wish that every year may be your **Best Year Ever!**

You now have the tools to **Make it Happen!**

# APPENDIX ONE

# QUICK TIPS, IDEAS AND ACTIVITIES

# IDEAS AND ACTIVITIES

1. BEHAVIOR REPORTS
2. BEST OF "BEST YEAR EVER!" LIST
3. "BEST YEAR EVER!" STUDENTS' BROCHURE
4. "BEST YEAR EVER!" VISUALIZATION ACTIVITY *
5. BRAIN WARM-UP ACTIVITIES *
   - Name Three
   - Brain Warm-Up Puzzle
   - Quote Of The Day
   - News Articles/News/Personal News
6. CASH IN WITH COIN CONNECTIONS *
   - Random Coin Checks
   - Symbolism Of Coin
7. DIVERSITY = STRONG TEAM *
8. END-OF-YEAR ACTIVITY
9. FUN (LIKE FUEL) FILLS THE TANK
10. GIVE CHOICES WHEN POSSIBLE
11. GREETINGS, GOOD-BYES, AND LOTS OF HIGH FIVES *
12. HIGH EXPECTATIONS
13. HUMOR
14. IDENTIFY OUR IDENTITIES *
15. STUDENTS PLAN AND RUN CLASSROOM PARTIES
16. MINI-GOALS
17. NAME STICKS IN A CUP

18.   NUMBERS *

19.   NO TRASH TALK TOLERATED

20.   100TH DAY CELEBRATION

21.   ONE-ON-ONE IN ONE

22.   OPEN MIKE/SHOW-AND-TELL SHARING
      EXPERIENCES

23.   PARENT INVOLVEMENT

24.   PRAISE/RECOGNITION/VALIDATION

25.   READ TO YOUR STUDENTS

26.   REPETITION, REPETITION, REPETITION

27.   REWARDS

      ◆ Team Awards

      ◆ Team Assist Awards

28    RULES WORKSHOP *

29.   SUCCESS STORIES

      ◆ Success Stories of the Rich And Famous

      ◆ Success Stories from the People Next Door

30.   TEAM CHALLENGES

31.   TEAM GOALS *

32.   TEAM RECORDS

33.   "TEAM" VS. "OUR CLASS" *

34.   TOSS A BALL

35.   USE OFFICE SPARINGLY

36.   WIN-WIN SITUATION

* Activities you should use early in the year.

# OVERVIEW

Most of the ideas and activities I list in this section, take only a few minutes out of your day, but produce big results if used consistently over time. They're easy to learn and easy to use.

Hopefully, you'll find a number of ideas and activities that you can take into your classroom and start using with your students. Play with them, alter them and do whatever you need to make them work for you and your students.

# BEHAVIOR REPORTS

**PURPOSE:** To hold students accountable while giving parents updates on how their child is doing in following our classroom rules during the times between conferences and report cards.

**TIME:** It takes about thirty minutes to fill out a class set of these reports.

**FREQUENCY:** Send home at the end of each month.

**SET-UP:**

1.  I keep a record during the month, that documents students who have broken class rules and the rules they have broken.

    **NOTE:** I keep a notebook on my desk to record this information. When a student breaks one of the classroom rules that are posted in the front of the room, I'll tell that student I'm going to put their name in my notebook, record which rule they broke, and what I expect them to do to get back on track.

    I do this without making any fuss or letting the incident become a distraction to whatever activity we're engaged in. My goal is to not embarrass the student, but to let that student know that one must be accountable for their actions.

    Since I have only five rules in my classroom, I record a student's name in the notebook, along with the day's date and the number of the rule they've broken. That saves time by not having to write out the rule itself.

2.  At the end of the month, I go through the notebook for that month, filling out a Behavior Report for each student. (See page 154 for a blank Behavior Report form.)

**Example:** Let's say I have a student named Beth, who had her name recorded in my notebook three times during the month—once for not following directions, and twice for talking at inappropriate times.

Under the heading, "Rules Mastering to Date," I would write down the number(s) of the rules that I did not write for her in my notebook for that month.

However, under the heading, "Rules to Continue Working On," I would write down the two numbers that represent the rules she has broken, and under the heading labeled, "Comments," I may write a brief comment explaining that neither of these are major concerns.

3. If a student completes the month without having their name recorded in my notebook for breaking a rule, I'll draw a star at the top of their Behavior Report, which they can later show to me to receive a small treat.

**NOTE:** Giving them a star and a small treat for a good report rewards them for their effort and helps to motivate them to complete the next month without having their name written down in the notebook.

Tell your students to take their Behavior Report home to be signed by an adult.

Give them a few days to get their reports signed and returned to you.

Remind your students at the start of each month that you are turning to a new page in your notebook and that they have the opportunity to start fresh for the month.

**NOTE:** I start each school year passing these out once a month. However, I usually stop sending them home somewhere in the middle of the school year, because most students have mastered our rules and no longer need this monthly reminder.

(Behavior Report Form)

# BEHAVIOR REPORT

**Student's Name**_____

**Date**_____

**Classroom Rules:**

1. Listen to and follow all directions the first time.

2. Come to class with all materials, a positive attitude and give good effort. Be a positive team member.

3. Use good manners when others are talking. Raise your hand; be an active listener.

4. Treat other people, their belongings and school property with respect. Be kind.

5. Work during work periods and use free time wisely. Complete and turn in assignments on time.

**Rules Mastering to Date:**

**Rules to Continue Working on:**

**Comments:**

**Parent's Signature:**

(Sample of Filled-in Behavior Report)

# BEHAVIOR REPORT

**Student's Name:** *Beth C.*

**Date:** *9/30/06*

**Classroom Rules:**

1. Listen to and follow all directions the first time.

2. Come to class with all materials, a positive attitude, and give good effort. Be a positive team member.

3. Use good manners when others are talking. Raise your hand; be an active listener.

4. Treat other people, their belongings, and school property with respect. Be kind.

5. Work during work periods, and use free time wisely. Complete and turn in assignments on time.

**Rules Mastering To Date:**

*2,4,5,6  Excellent effort, Beth! Keep it going!*

**Rules To Continue Working On:**

*1,3*

**Comments:**

*Beth is doing very well learning and mastering our classroom rules. She has needed only a couple of reminders for rules 1 and 3. I think she will have these mastered by the next report at the end of October.*

**Parent's Signature:**

## BEST OF "BEST YEAR EVER!" LIST

At the end of the school year, tell your students to brainstorm a list of their favorite activities, projects, assignments, memories and stories from the year to help remind you of what to keep around to use with your students next year.

Keep this list in your lesson plan book and find time to work at least some of these "best of" activities into your plans. Be sure to let your current students know that an activity that made your list was chosen as a favorite by your last year's group. This helps give the activity more credibility before your students even begin working on it.

**Idea:** When you have your group help generate a list of their favorite activities for you to use with your next year's group, record their responses on large chart paper that you can pull out and show your next year's group of students. Depending on the size of the list, this can send a strong, silent message to your new students that they're going to be doing a lot of cool things in the upcoming year.

## "BEST YEAR EVER!" STUDENTS' BROCHURE

**PURPOSE:** Having my students create their own brochure is a great end-of-the-year activity that encourages your students to reflect on their best year ever and the highlights of being in your classroom. Also, this can be a great way of finding out how much of this they're going to take with them when they leave on the last day of school.

**Example:** This reminds me of throwing spaghetti on the wall to see if it's done. If the spaghetti sticks to the wall, it's done. This brochure is a chance to see how much of what you've been talking about this year with regard to *Best Year Ever!* has stuck in their memory. The more they stick in their brochure, the more successful you've been with this program.

**CLASS OBJECTIVE:** The objective is to create a set of brochures that will clearly explain to next year's class what *Best Year Ever!* means and what they can expect and look forward to as a student from this teacher at this grade level.

**TIME:** 1-2 weeks—with students mostly working on these during free time in class and at home.

**SET-UP:**

1. Before you introduce this activity, you may want to come up with a checklist you can give to the kids to follow as a road map of what needs to be included in their brochures.

---

### Sample Checklist for Best Year Ever! Brochure:

**All Brochures Must Include ____# Of The Following:**

- ☑ Best Year Ever! Coin
- ☑ Favorite Signs Around Room
- ☑ Activities Related to Best Year Ever!
- ☑ Team Goals
- ☑ Working as a Team
- ☑ Favorite Memories From Our Room
- ☑ Describe Teacher
- ☑ What Next Year's Students Need to do to Have *Their* Best Year Ever!
- ☑ The Classroom
- ☑ What Makes Our Room Unique/Special
- ☑ Diversity = Strong Team
- ☑ Include at Least Three Illustrations

---

2.  Decide before you introduce the activity whether you're going to allow kids to work together in small groups, in pairs or work individually on this project.

3.  To introduce this activity, I tell the kids that I want to create a brochure that I can give to my next-year students which will explain to them what *Best Year Ever!* means, and what they can expect life to be like as a student in my classroom.

4.  Another good idea is to ask the kids to brainstorm their own list of information/ideas of things that should be included in the brochure.

    **NOTE:** I would probably ask them to think back over the year in silence for a few minutes to allow time for them to generate their own list of ideas based on their reflections, and then I would ask them to share some of their responses with a learning partner or group members before trying to attempt a class list.

5.  I tell the kids they're going to do a project where they'll create a brochure for next year's students to read on the very first day of school. The brochure will explain all about *Best Year Ever!* and life as a student in your classroom.

6.  Give each child a set of guidelines or checklist and carefully go over each item on it with your class, explaining what you're hoping to see in their brochures.

7.  Challenge them to give their best effort to show the new students *coming* to this grade level what students *leaving* this grade level are capable of doing. "Amaze them with your work!"

    **Idea:** You could have a contest to see who can design and create the best brochure. Winners could have first dibs on things you're getting rid of at the end of the year or some other prize they'd be motivated to try to win.

8.  Encourage them to do a rough draft that their parents must read before you give them the okay—and the paper/materials—to start their final product. Allow them to use a computer for part or all of their brochure if they choose.

    NOTE: I've found, through experience, that it's a good idea to ban magic markers and crayons on this project. The projects come out looking neater and more professional if they use colored pencils.

9.  If possible, ask each of them to make a quick web or word list of what they'd like to include in their brochure while their enthusiasm is high.

10. Allow time and encourage kids to share what they are doing and give them a chance to give and receive some feedback—especially during the rough-draft phase.

    Idea: During the last week of school, when I'm done collecting grades and I've collected all their books, I spend a lot of class time cleaning, reorganizing and putting things away for the year. This is a great time to let kids work on this activity during class time.

11. When brochures are finished, give kids a chance to share them with each other. This is a great way to reminisce about your group's best year ever.

12. Put these brochures in a safe spot until next year, and pull them out the first day of school the following year to help introduce your new students to their best year ever and to your room.

    NOTE: When your new students read these brochures created by old students, they'll hear about the room from another student's point-of-view.

# "BEST YEAR EVER!"
# VISUALIZATION ACTIVITIES

**PURPOSE:** To encourage every student to attach a strong personal image or feeling to the slogan, *Best Year Ever!* Whenever they hear or read this slogan, they can clearly see in their mind's eye what they're working to attain this year.

**TIME:** 30-40 minutes

## SET-UP:

1.  Share with your students examples of how top athletes like Jack Nicklaus, Tiger Woods, and Michael Jordan have used visualization techniques to help focus on a desired outcome to enhance their performance in each of their sports.

    **Example:** Tiger Woods, when asked what he thinks about before each shot, responded that he visualizes where he wants the ball to go instead of where he doesn't want it to land. Explain to your students that it's important for them to have a clear image and feeling in their mind of what *Best Year Ever!* means to them, so that this slogan can have more of a powerful, positive impact on them throughout the year.

2.  Instruct your students to take a minute or two of silence and concentrate on what they visualize and feel whenever they think about *Best Year Ever!* or what having their best year ever looks and feels like.

3.  Take two to three minutes and let the kids share with the rest of the class what they see, feel, and think about when they hear or read the slogan, *Best Year Ever!*

4.  Ask the students to write a brief journal entry about what that slogan means to them and their images and feelings

when they hear, read or think about *Best Year Ever!* (5-10 minutes)

5.  After the kids have finished writing about this topic, ask each of them to share what they wrote with members of their group by reading aloud from their journal.

6.  You may want to ask each group to choose one person in their group to share what they wrote with the rest of the class. I usually ask them to pick one that they thought was really interesting, different or really stood out when they heard it.

7.  Give the kids another two or three minutes to add anything or make any changes they wish before putting away their journals.

8.  Stress to your students the importance of remembering what they wrote in their journals and to visualize or think about what they wrote whenever they hear, read or see the slogan, *Best Year Ever!*

9.  Explain how—by doing this on a regular basis—this will help to keep them moving in the right direction to reach this goal by the end of the year.

10. Remind your students that they have the freedom to change or build upon their thoughts, feelings and images that they attached to the *Best Year Ever!* slogan.

    **NOTE:** This is something you may want to revisit at least once a semester to allow the kids to change their choices, if they desire, and to reinforce the idea and importance of attaching a clear, positive image or feeling to this slogan.

**Idea:** When the kids come in after lunch, have them take two minutes to silently reflect on what *Best Year Ever!* means to them and to visualize themselves having their best year ever. This is a great way to calm them down and help to create a positive mind-set for the afternoon.

## BRAIN WARM-UP ACTIVITIES

Each morning, I start off the first 20-25 minutes of the day with a wake-up time called "Brain Warm-up," which is my favorite time of the day. It's filled with a number of mini-activities that help promote a more positive way to approach one's day. This also allows me time to reset the table for success each day before trying to serve the "meal" for the day.

Along with the activities I'm about to share, this time is also used to take care of some classroom business, like watering the plants, feeding and getting water for our pet tarantula, taking attendance and our lunch count.

The kids also use this time as a quiet work time. Once they write out the agenda/schedule for the day, they may use this time each morning to work on ongoing projects, complete and double check all homework due that day, draw or just sit and listen to any discussions or sharing taking place in our room.

**NOTE:** By allowing kids to work on any unfinished work during this time, I've cut down on the number of late assignments. More and more, lately, I've noticed a large increase in the number of evening activities in which my students are involved or in which their siblings are participating which they must attend. This period allows them to use their time wisely to get caught up.

## Activity One: Name Three

**PURPOSE:** To urge students to focus on the positive things going on in their life, and help them build a habit of being able to identify the good things going on around them.

**STEPS TO FOLLOW:**

1.  At the start of each morning, ask your students to write down three things they're excited, happy or proud of. These things don't have to be big in their life. They can be little things such as excitement/pleasure about the cereal they ate for breakfast that morning.

2.  Remind them to write three new things each day. You can even challenge them to see how many days they can go without repeating anything on their list.

    **NOTE:** By not repeating things on their list, they'll hopefully start to realize that they have a lot of things to be happy and thankful for in their lives.

3.  During the first few days, ask them to share what they wrote with their group members to help spark ideas the others can use on their own lists. You may even ask for volunteers to share one of the items on their list with the whole class. Again, this may help remind other kids of things they can add to their lists in the days to come.

4.  After the first few days, ask the kids to share items on their list a few times each month to let them know you're still interested in how they're doing with this.

5.  Once a month, or a few times during the year, you could put a large sheet of chart paper on a wall and have them write one thing they wrote on their list during the past month that they really want to share for others to read; or ask them to write something about which they're happy, excited or proud of, in terms of what's going on in your classroom.

### The Rationale Behind "Name Three"

I post a sign with a quote on our current events bulletin board that reads, "The Way You Choose to See the World Creates the World You See."

The quote reminds everyone in my classroom that *you see what you focus on!* If you focus on all the bad in the world, you'll see the world as a bad, scary place. If you focus on all the good in the world, you'll see the world as a good place.

Early in the year, I ask the kids to do the following exercise to help make this point:

**Exercise:** Ask everyone to focus on a certain color in the room and then ask them to name everything that is that color in the room. They'll start to see items with that color all over the place. Next, ask them to focus on another color—let's say yellow—and, then, tell them to close their eyes and name everything in the room that's red. It will be hard for them to name anything that color because they had been focusing on yellow.

I tell the kids that the same is true with what they decide to focus on in their life and world. If they only focus on the bad things happening in their lives, that's all they'll see.

However, the same is true if they learn to focus on all the good going on around them. They'll tend to see mostly good things in their life and world.

I have a true story about a women I observed early one morning while waiting in line to pay for some gasoline. I watched this woman frantically digging in her purse trying to scratch together enough change to pay for her cigarettes. She was mumbling and grumbling as she searched. She finally gathered enough change, paid the clerk, and quickly exited the store, blurting, "It's going to be one of those days!"

She'd already decided, *before 7:15 A.M.*, what she was going to focus on that day and what kind of day she expected to have. I remind the kids that *they'll see what they focus on.* It's *their* choice!

## Activity Two: Brain Warm-Up Puzzle

**PURPOSE:** At the beginning of the year, I use this activity to help kids work on their problem-solving skills and their ability to look at problems and puzzles in more than one way. Around the end of winter, I start using this activity more often to strengthen our team unity.

**MATERIALS:** Start collecting a file full of brain teasers, word and math puzzles. You can find many types of puzzles in bookstores, newspapers, magazines and on the Internet.

**STEPS TO FOLLOW:**

1.  Find a place in the classroom where you can post a puzzle each day for all to see.

    **Example:** I use a small portion of my chalkboard. I write the title, "Brain Warm-up" and put the puzzle underneath.

2.  Put the puzzle up before your students come in for the morning. For some, this will become one of their first stops upon entering your room.

    **Puzzle #1:** It's a freezing night, and you finally reach the mountain cabin you've rented for the weekend. The electricity has been knocked out, and there are no lights and no heat. There's a fireplace with a stack of wood in it, a wood-burning stove, an oil lamp and a gray candle. You search your pockets and find that you have a single wooden match. You look at the resources you have available. What will you light first?

    **Answer:** the match

**Puzzle #2:** If Tom is twice as old as Howard will be when Joe is as old as Tom is now, who is the oldest, the next oldest and the youngest?

> **Answer:** Tom is oldest, Howard is middle, Joe is youngest.

3. Read the brain warm-up first thing in the morning and tell them you'll call on someone after lunch to answer it.

4. Ask them not to tell anyone else the answer if they solve it.

5. Tell them to write the answers in a notebook if they'd like to start a collection of these to try out on family members and friends.

   **NOTE:** Early in the year, I encourage my students to write these down and try to stump their parents and older siblings. I tell them to wait until everyone is sitting around the table for dinner so they have an audience when they show everyone how smart they are. This is all done in fun. My goal is to get them talking about our classroom and school during dinner.

6. Ask kids to silently work on the puzzles during this brain warm-up time each morning.

7. After lunch, start the afternoon by asking your students whether anyone knows the answer and letting them make their guesses. When a child makes a guess, tell them to explain and show how they came up with that answer. If someone gets the correct answer, really praise them to help motivate more students to participate in the future.

   **NOTE:** I don't grade these in any way. They're used strictly as fun and to try to motivate the kids to take some risks, learn that it's okay to make mistakes, and try to learn from them.

8. If no one gets the correct answer, you may want to leave the puzzle up for a day or two longer to see if they can get it. If

they think you'll just give them the answer, many of the kids won't feel the need to try too hard to figure out the answer.

**EXTENSION ACTIVITY:** Somewhere between the middle and the end of the year, you can use the brain-warm-up puzzle as a way to focus on "all involved." Set it up so that each day the brain warm-up puzzle must be correctly solved in order for the class to earn recess.

Tell the kids that after lunch you'll randomly select one student to answer the brain warm-up puzzle. They must be able to come up and solve the puzzle correctly and show the class how to solve it. If they're able to do both parts correctly, then they'll earn the class its recess.

If they can't solve the problem, tell them they may call on a friend to help them. If they can solve it with a friend, they earn one-half recess for the class.

Before I select someone to solve the problem, I give the class about five minutes to work together to make sure everyone in the room knows the answer and can show the steps needed to solve it.

This tends to highly motivate the kids to try to solve the puzzle on their own *before* lunch and then to work together after lunch to make sure everyone learns how to answer the puzzle correctly.

## Activity Three: Quote Of The Day

**PURPOSE:** To motivate and provide students with some nutritional food for thought.

**MATERIALS:** Start a file of inspirational quotes that relate to *Best Year Ever!* or any other quotes relating to personal growth.

**NOTE:** There are many books available full of famous, thought-provoking quotes. To save you some time searching for quotes to use in your classroom each day, I've included a year's supply of quotes in the back of this book for you to use. (See *Appendix 3*.)

## STEPS TO FOLLOW:

Each day, before school, select a quote and put it up on the board. Tell the kids to write the quote down so they can keep a running collection of them.

**Example:** I tell the kids to write the quote in their Agenda Book so they can remember what we're focusing on that day. Also, I'm hoping that these quotes will catch their parents' attention once in while, and lead to a discussion of what we're talking about in class.

After you go over the agenda/schedule and read the brain warm-up, read the quote aloud and give the students two minutes to talk in their groups about what they think the quote means and how they think it pertains to having their best year ever.

After two minutes of small-group discussions, call on volunteers to explain to the class what the quote means to them and how they think it pertains to the class.

**NOTE:** It's important to accept their interpretation even if it doesn't exactly fit your own. Many times they will come up with a better interpretation than mine!

Next, explain to the class what the quote means to you, making as many connections as you can to *Best Year Ever!*

**Extension Activity #1:** Don't be surprised if your students start coming to you with quotes and brain warm-up puzzles to share with the class. This is a great way to get them all involved.

Ask them to write the quote or puzzle on a piece of paper and check it out yourself to make sure it's appropriate for your class. If it meets your standards, arrange for them to put it up one day during the week.

They will be the one to read it to the class and call on students to respond or answer it. You'll find the kids get a real charge out of this, and take it seriously. Also, realize that it will most likely take only one student to open the flood gates. Once one child goes through this process, many more will follow.

**Extension Activity #2:** Have your students write the quote down each day and write for three minutes about what they think the quote means to them and how it relates to them working as a team to have their best year ever. Have them write immediately following your class discussion.

After they write for three minutes, pair them up and have them read their responses to each other. Finally, randomly choose three students to read their written responses to the entire class followed by you sharing *your* written response with your class.

## Activity Four: News Articles, News, Personal News

**PURPOSE:** To provide a more balanced view of what's going on than television programs and news media sometimes present, and keep them in touch with what's going on around the world, in our country, your state, city, neighborhood and your students' lives.

**STEPS TO FOLLOW:**

*PART ONE: Before Starting Activity with Kids*

If possible, create a bulletin board where you can post articles about current events.

**Example:** The bulletin board in the back of my room is about six feet long. A large, orange, sun-shaped sign at the top of the board reads: "The Way You Choose to See the World Creates the World You See"

At the bottom of the bulletin board is a picture of a small portion of the world that runs the length of the board, while the middle of the board is covered with yellow butcher paper. The articles are stapled between the sun and the world onto this yellow paper.

Cut out a few articles and staple them onto the board. Try to find at least one story that's reporting on something positive.

### PART TWO: Introducing This Activity to Kids

1. Introduce this activity to your students by giving them a chance to discuss what usually makes front-page news and opening stories on television news programs.

2. Ask your students how they think a visitor to our country would feel about America—or your city—even if they only read the front page of a national newspaper like *USA Today* or watched the first ten minutes of your city's local news broadcast on television.

   **NOTE:** Most of these stories cover natural disasters, tragedies, crimes and scandals. This would probably give most visitors the wrong impression of what life in the United States is really like. Visitors may feel that they're not going to be safe in our country because of all the bad happenings they hear about.

3. Explain to your students how newspapers and news programs do not usually provide a balanced view/perspective of what's going on around the country—or your city.

4. Ask your students, "If this isn't a balanced view of what is really going on, why does the news media consistently focus on those types of stories?"

**NOTE:** This is a great place to discuss how the news media is trying to sell news that's exciting so more people will buy their papers or watch their broadcasts and buy their sponsors' products.

Invite students to bring articles to share with the class during this time each morning throughout the year, and challenge them to bring in articles that show a more balanced picture of what is really taking place in our world.

**Example:** In my classroom, I ask the kids to follow the guidelines listed below when bringing in an article.

- one article per day
- should know what the article is about
- has permission to bring in article
- news article should be recent

**NOTE:** You may want to offer a little incentive for kids to bring articles. I give a child a sticker for each article they bring in to put on their Agenda Book. I ask the kids to keep track to see who has collected the most stickers.

If not enough "good-news stories" are coming in, I will offer a small piece of candy for each story brought in about someone helping someone else.

## PART THREE: Daily Running of Activity

1. After you've taken attendance, introduced the brain warm-up, and have discussed the quote of the day, ask the students to raise their hands if they brought in a news article.

2. Ask each student to briefly explain what their article is about before you read it to the class.

   **NOTE:** I suggest you skim through the article as you read, pulling out the important parts of the article to read to the kids. You can edit out parts of the article that you feel would not be appropriate for your class to hear.

3. Take time between articles to have mini-discussions, if you feel the article contained something worth clarifying, talking about or debating.

   **NOTE:** Put the articles up on the news board sometime during the same day. Assign students to take old articles off the bulletin board at least once a month.

4. Once you've read all the articles, ask the class if anyone has any "news-news" to share.

   **NOTE:** I define news-news as any news they've heard about through watching television or listening to the radio. It cannot be personal news, and they have to have a pretty clear understanding about the details of the story to be able to share it with the class. For example, they cannot share with the class that they heard that a plane crashed somewhere and they think some people may have gotten hurt. This story is too vague. They should know the basic who, what, where, when and why.

5. Encourage kids to bring in articles discussed during news-news, especially the more interesting stories.

6. Finally, if time allows, tell the kids to raise their hands if they have something important happening in their personal lives that they'd like to share with the class.

   **NOTE:** If you're pressed for time and a lot of kids want to share, ask them to share their news in one sentence.

This is a great way to learn more about each student and find out what's important to them. It also teaches them to get to the heart of a story about anything, whether it's media news or something from their own lives.

7. Be sure to share some personal news and stories of your own with your students. They love that!

Example: I share a lot of my life with the kids through stories. I'll tell them funny stories about growing up, and about my life as an adult. Most of the stories are used to help target-talk about something I want them to think about in terms of their own lives. However, some are just told to let them know I care about them enough to include them in something that is very special to me—my family. Hopefully, showing them a more human side of me helps to break down the "us vs. them" mentality that sometimes exists between students and teachers.

## CASH IN WITH COIN CONNECTIONS

Here are a couple of ideas that can help make the *Best Year Ever!* coin a more valuable tool for you and your students to use in your classroom throughout the year.

### Random Coin Checks

Every so often, pull a name stick out of the cup. If that student can present their coin—from their desk, pocket, backpack or locker—give the class a few extra minutes of recess or some other fun treat. The kid who presents the coin becomes an instant hero.

This also encourages students to bring their coins to school every day and to take good care of them.

*Story: At the beginning of one school year, I gave my former superintendent a coin, explaining my Best Year Ever! program to him. He was a big fan of this idea. About a month later, he was walking past my classroom and popped in to say hello. I introduced him to the class—and he pulled out his coin to show us that he carries his around! I told him that by showing me his coin, he had just earned the kids ten extra minutes of recess that day. He immediately got a huge applause from twenty-four very excited students. Obviously, he got a kick out of that.*

*I didn't realize how much he appreciated that until a couple months later when I saw him outside our office and waved to him. He walked over to me and we started talking. As we walked back toward my classroom, he was disappointed to find my room empty and asked me where my students were. I explained that they were at PE. He reached in his pocket, pulled out the coin, and told me he wanted to earn the kids another bonus recess.*

*The first time he presented the coin to the class it had such a positive impact on him that he wanted to do it again. I knew at that moment that the idea of doing random coin checks was a winner.*

*As an old commercial says, "Try It—You'll Like It!" So will your students.*

## Symbolism of the Coin

The coin symbolizes many things. How you use the coin and tie the coin into what you're talking about will determine how many different symbols the coin will hold for your students.

Hold the coin in your hand whenever you are talking about *Best Year Ever!*, and the kids will begin to equate the coin with the slogan/idea. Similarly, the American Flag makes you think of the United States whenever you see it waving on a flagpole. Someone doesn't have to be whispering in your ear, "United States," for you to make that connection.

Hopefully, the same thing will begin to happen with the coin. You'll help your students make the connection—so many times—that eventually, whenever your students see or hold their coin, they'll be thinking about *Best Year Ever!* and what it means to them.

The following is a list of times I'll hold the coin to help them make the *Best Year Ever!* connection:

◆ Greeting each child as they enter the room each morning.

◆ During my introductory remarks each morning— especially when I say, "Good morning, and welcome to day # __ of what you are still working on to be your best year ever."

◆ Whenever I'm telling them how much I appreciate their work or behavior.

◆ Waiting at the front of the line waiting for everyone to finish lining up before going to another class.

◆ Wrapping up the day and waiting to dismiss kids before the bell rings.

The coin should also be a symbol for the three words—Attendance, Attitude and Effort—on the back of the coin. The coin should be an automatic reminder for the kids to give more (or their best) effort and to keep a positive attitude. Again, the more you can connect the coin to these three words at the beginning of the year, the stronger the symbol will become.

The following are some examples of making the above connection using the coin:

◆ Talking about attendance.

◆ Giving instructions for an assignment/project.

◆ Asking them to give a guest speaker or another teacher their full attention.

◆ Stating expectations for working together on a class or group assignment/project.

**Story #1:** *I knew the coin was starting to have real meaning for my students during our MEAP test (Michigan Educational Assessment Program). During the test, a number of students had their coins out on their desks—so much so, that a proctor helping to administer the test noticed and asked me what they were.*

*Later, I asked the students why they had their coins out. They said it was to remind them to give their best effort. I thought this was cool because it showed me they were able to make this connection, and they were doing it on their own.*

*One student told me he doesn't need to look at his coin anymore, because when he needs it, he can just visualize in his mind what it looks like and that reminds him to give more effort when needed.*

**Story #2:** *I gave our former librarian, a good friend, a Best Year Ever! coin as a gift. I was surprised during my class's first visit to the library that she held it in her hand—never once referring to it—while teaching her lesson. Every student in my room noticed the coin. She was sending each student a message that she's aware of what we as a class are working on and that she's supporting us with her effort and attitude.*

*She continued to have the coin out every time she worked with my group, and they responded by giving her their best effort.*

The coin can also become a symbol for your team. Like a team banner or a uniform, the coin can begin to represent your class and what you are working to achieve.

## DIVERSITY = STRONG TEAM

A good beginning-of-the-year discussion with your new students is to explain how a team made up of individuals who are different will have more strengths than a team where everyone is exactly alike.

Use the following example—or come up with one you're more comfortable with—to help make the above statement clear to all your students.

Example: Imagine playing on a soccer team where everyone is exactly alike. For example, imagine every person on your team is an all-star goalie. Your team would be almost impossible to score on.

However, you probably wouldn't win very many games, because your team wouldn't be able to score very many goals. A team of all-star goalies wouldn't have the skills needed to put the ball in the back of their opponent's net.

Good teams are made up of players with different interests, abilities, shapes and sizes. Some players are fast and small and can fly down the wings, blowing past the other team's defenders. Some players are tall and good at jumping, which enables them to go up and head balls smaller players can't reach. Some players can tap dance on the ball, dribbling through a forest of players untouched, and some players have a cannon for a foot and can blast shots toward the other team's goal.

If you had your choice to play on a team where everyone was exactly alike or on a team where everyone was different and had different things to bring to the team, I'll bet many of you would choose the latter—the team with lots of diversity.

Diversity makes a team strong, and we're a team working together to have our best year ever, so we want plenty of diversity in our room. We all have things in common—like working to have our best year ever—but it's our *differences* that will make us strong. Therefore, this year we will celebrate the diversity in our room.

Take time with your students to find and identify examples of diversity in your room, and discuss ways that will make your team stronger.

## END OF YEAR ACTIVITY

To help summarize the main ideas behind *Best Year Ever!* and to remind your students that it will now become their responsibility to go forth and continue to strive to make each year their best year ever, read the book, *Knots on a Counting Rope,* by Bill Martin, Jr. and John Archambault, illustrated by Ted Rand, to your students.

Before you start reading, ask your students to listen for ways the story connects with your year-long theme of *Best Year Ever!*

NOTE: This is a story about a little boy learning to live his life to its fullest—despite being born with no sight—with the help of his loving grandfather. The grandfather, through many re-tellings, is trying to help his grandson remember the story about how the boy was able to see past his blindness to clearly visualize his dreams and make them a reality so that the little boy will be able to carry on the tradition of telling the story after the grandfather has died.

After you finish reading the story, ask your students to share any connections they were able to make between the story and the coin and *Best Year Ever!* There are a lot of metaphors throughout the story, so you'll probably need to ask specific questions to help guide them at first.

Following is a list of connections you may want to ask your students to make:

◆ Little Boy = Students

◆ Birth of Little Boy = Attendance

◆ Blue Horses = Effort and Attitude

◆ Dark Mountains = Obstacles and Self-Defeating Habits

◆ Blindness = Fear of the Unknown

◆ Blue = Hope, Happiness and Faith in Self

◆ Horse Race = Tests and Personal Challenges

◆ Counting Rope = The Coin and Memories of This Past Year

◆ Grandfather = You (Teacher)

**NOTE:** Let the kids make as many connections as they can before you start sharing your own.

At the end of this discussion time, tell them that, like the grandfather, you will not be going with them to the next grade level. It's now their turn to remember the story of their best year ever and to be able to tell it to themselves from this point on.

Remind them that the coin is like their very own counting rope from the story. It can help to remind them of all the powerful messages and memories they experienced during the year. It can always remind them that they now have the tools to make every situation and year their best year ever.

# FUN (LIKE FUEL) FILLS THE TANK

Make it a goal to model for your students that working hard can be fun, and that when you're having fun, it helps you to work harder. Focus on having fun with your students, and teach them how to harness that energy into working harder.

From my own experiences, I realize that I tend to give more time and effort to those things I enjoy—like playing with my son, rehearsing for a play and working on this project. However, I tend to rush through and just give enough effort to those things I don't enjoy—like making my bed, paying the bills and doing yard work.

Therefore, I come to work expecting to have fun. I'm constantly looking for new ways to present the curriculum to my students so boredom doesn't set in. That's how I gauge things in my room. If I'm doing too much of the same things, I get bored teaching, *and I know that if I'm bored the kids must be bored.*

Granted, not everything can be fun or made exciting, but I believe the kids are more willing to work through those assignments knowing that something more interesting or fun will be coming down the pike soon enough.

If you haven't done so already, adopt the *Highlights* magazine's mission statement for your classroom: "Fun with a Purpose." Your students will appreciate the fact that you're working hard to find ways to make their learning experience more fun, which is another way you can show them you care about them. Don't be surprised if they start working harder for you.

Last, what great modeling you're providing—showing your students that as an adult in the workplace, you can really enjoy yourself while working hard to get the job done.

## GIVE CHOICES WHEN POSSIBLE

Find times during your day where the kids can decide best how to use their own time. Most kids will take advantage of this time to get their work done so they don't have as much homework.

> **Example:** I'll read to my students for the first twenty minutes after lunch a few times during the week. During this activity, I allow them to choose how they want to use their time. They can draw, work on other projects, read or just sit and listen. I also give them this choice each morning during our brain warm-up time.

This creates a win-win situation in your classroom. Your students win because they feel they have some control in their work day, which is important to them. They also have more opportunities to get their work done so they don't have to deal with late assignments and falling behind in your classroom. This is especially true for a student who's been absent.

You win because you don't have to deal with as many late assignments. The quality of students' work should also increase, because they're not as rushed to get it done. You can also assign mini-projects for the kids to work on during the week, knowing they have this time to complete them.

> **Idea:** Ask your students to take spelling words and characters from stories you're reading and construct a comic strip, which will be due at the end of the week. This assignment will give them something to do during these free-choice times while giving them a novel way to study and use their spelling words for the week.

As long as kids are getting their work done, don't get upset if they don't choose to work during this time. They're most likely doing what they need to do to better prepare themselves for the rest of the day.

## GREETINGS AND GOODBYES

Customer service is the most overlooked aspect in our business. Many stores will spend lots of money advertising their products, building and maintaining a beautiful place to shop, and will work to give their customers a good product at a competitive price, but spend little time and energy on training their employees to better serve customers' needs while in their store. Unfortunately, I'm sure we've all had bad experiences with less-than-gracious store employees and wait staff in restaurants. They treated us as though we were unimportant, in their way, or the cause of their discomfort. However they treated us, it tainted our shopping or dining experience and possibly made us swear we would never go back.

Take a second and remember a time where you were shopping or out to eat and you received excellent service. My guess is that—even now—it brings back a good feeling. Your experience at their business was very positive and you felt encouraged to patronize that business again. You also felt motivated to tell others, which is great advertising for the business.

Schools, for the most part, don't work hard enough to provide that kind of experience for their students and their parents. Parents are now being given more and more choices about where they can send their children to be educated. Schools, therefore, need to rethink their "customer-service" policy.

Hopefully, your approach to customer service is geared around the Golden Rule, which reminds you to treat others the way you want to be treated. This activity will help make your classroom soar above the rest.

Take time every morning to greet your kids as they walk into the room. Stand by the door and greet each child with a "Hello," "Good morning" or some other positive comment. I usually look for new outfits and haircuts and comment on them.

At first, don't be surprised or hurt if your kids don't respond. They'll probably be in shock, because few teachers, if any, have ever done this for them. It won't take long for them to become comfortable with it and even look forward to your greeting. You'll have a chance to say something positive to each student before they even set foot in your room to start the day.

> **NOTE:** I know this means a lot to the kids, because I hear about it on those few occasions when I'm unable to fulfill this morning ritual.

Do the same thing at the end of the day. Stand at the door after you dismiss the kids for the day and say goodbye to each student as they walk out. No matter what happened between you and a particular student during the day, this is a good opportunity to end it on a positive note.

> **Idea:** Don't be afraid to give your team high fives as they walk out the door. This type of physical contact is quick, appropriate and powerful. It is one more way to break down that "us vs. them" barrier that too often exists between teacher and students.

When you walk your kids to gym, music or lunch, take that opportunity to tell them they've done a nice job so far that day, that you hope they'll have fun at their next activity or that you'll see them in a little while. Make sure you get a chance to say something to each child, or at least look each kid in the eye as you say whatever you choose to say to the group.

This will help show the kids that you do care about them and should help to build a strong bond between you and your group.

# HIGH EXPECTATIONS

Set high expectations for your students—individually and as a team. Remind them often that a big part of achieving their best year ever is to constantly strive to be the best they can be. It's not about being perfect. It's about challenging themselves to be better than they are now—always willing to take risks and learn from their mistakes.

As the old saying goes: "Expect the Best—Get the Best!"

# HUMOR

Use humor in your classroom like a good chef uses seasoning. If you use the right amount at the right time, it can really spice up your lesson. Tell your students that you'll use humor as often as they can handle it. If they get too silly or can't focus on the task, then pull back. However, if they can use it to work harder longer, keep it going.

> **NOTE:** Tell your students that humor is *never* funny if it comes at the expense of others, and it's important to never go for that kind of cheap laugh. Make sure to model the type of humor you feel is appropriate for the team.

# IDENTIFY OUR IDENTITIES

This is a great beginning-of-the-year activity that helps build the team and reinforce the concept: Diversity = Strong Team.

To help show how a team is made up of individuals with lots of commonalties and differences, ask each student to cut out pictures of things with which they identify from old magazines, and glue them into a collage that represents them.

> **Idea:** Before the kids cut pictures out of old magazines, ask them to create a list of things they like to do, like to eat, and any other things they can think of with which they strongly identify. Once that list is completed, turn it into a shopping list that will be used when looking through magazines to find pictures to cut out.

My shopping list would include some of the following:

| | |
|---|---|
| teaching | tacos |
| boating | family |
| tubing | fatherhood |
| water skiing | Chicago |
| theater | soccer |
| acting | Western Michigan |
| pizza | University |

When each child has created his or her own collage, arrange them together as one big collage on a large wall for others to see. Put a sign in the middle of this team collage that reads:  **"Identify Our Identities!"**

Tell your students that this collage represents how a group of individuals with many similarities and differences can come together to make a strong team.

> **Idea:** Leave this collage up long enough for parents to see it at your fall open house. Encourage your students to challenge their parents by asking them to identify their child's collage out of the larger team collage. Tell your kids it's a fun way to see how well their parents really know them.

This would also be a great time for your students to explain to their parents why you put all the collages together to make a team collage, and to tell their parents about how diversity on a team can make it stronger. Letting your students explain the collage to their parents helps them to lock in this concept and make it their own.

## KIDS PLAN AND RUN CLASSROOM PARTIES

This is a great idea to help involve everyone in sharing classroom celebrations. Instead of letting room mothers plan and run the parties, put this responsibility on your students and see how they respond. Parents are still invited to your parties, but with the understanding that they'll be treated like guests and won't be expected to work.

About a week before each party, ask your class to generate a list of possible food items they'd like to eat at the party. You may want to have different headings like sweets, healthy food and junk food, and then vote for one or two top selections under each.

Then select specific students to bring in the needed items for the party. You may want to give first selection choices to those students who have not had a chance to bring anything in for previous parties during the year. This helps to ensure that everyone has the opportunity to bring something in.

On the day of the party, let the kids who brought refreshments or other items be responsible for passing them out. Also, assign clean-up chores to volunteers who want to help.

Most parents seem to like this setup because everyone gets a chance to share instead of expecting certain parents to do all the work. Parents enjoy coming in for the party and being able to sit with other parents or their kids and participate in the fun.

# MINI-GOALS

**PURPOSE:** Each month, every kid sets a small, personal goal they'd like to achieve by the end of the month. This activity is designed to show them the power of writing down a goal and taking a little time each day to focus on that goal to increase their odds of achieving it. This approach can be used when setting larger, long-term goals.

**MATERIALS:** Note cards.

**TIME:** This activity takes about ten minutes on the first day of each month, when the kids are writing down their new goals. Each day during the month, you need only one minute for students to read and focus on their goal. The last day of the month, you'll need to allow about 10-15 minutes for kids to reflect on and share their success stories with each other.

**STEPS TO FOLLOW:**

1.  Tell the kids to think of a goal they'd like to accomplish by the end of the month.

    **NOTE:** Make sure the kids are setting realistic goals for this time frame and that they're setting goals they really want to accomplish. The goal can be related to school or to something they'd like to accomplish outside of school.

2.  Ask kids to share with the group what they plan to work on as their goal to help other students determine what they want to set as a goal.

3.  Give the kids the following formula to use when writing out their goals:

    Write the goal as if they're already doing it, a time limit to reach their goal, what they'll be doing to reach their goal, and what their goal will look like when they accomplish it.

*(Try to keep goals to 25 words or less.)*

**Example of a Goal:** In the next three weeks, I see myself practicing my musical instrument twenty minutes per night so I can get my practice card filled out.

4.  Give each child a note card so they can write out their goal.

5.  Ask the kids to read their goals to each other in their group, and then, choose a few students to read them to the whole class.

6.  Staple their cards to the outside cover of a notebook or folder that you know they'll be using each day in class.

7.  Each day, let them pull out their notebook or folder and take one minute to read their goal to themselves and then use the rest of the minute to visualize that goal as already accomplished or to think about what they're doing to reach it.

8.  At least once a week, ask the kids to raise their hands if they feel they're on track to accomplish their goal by the end of the month. You can even let them take two minutes in their group to discuss what they're doing each day to work toward their goal.

9.  After three to four weeks, check to see who has reached their goals and who didn't, and why. Again, let kids share in their groups how they performed and how they feel if they were able to reach their goal. Ask them to share some of their success stories with the rest of the class.

    **NOTE:** You may want to have a "wall of fame" where kids can put up the goals they've achieved throughout the year to help celebrate and reinforce their efforts to make their goals a reality.

10. Set new goals each month and repeat the process.

NOTE: I started setting goals with the kids to help model that I feel it's something worth doing. I share with the kids when I'm successful and when I'm not. I've learned from doing this activity that when I don't reach a goal, it is most likely due to the fact that I wasn't really excited about the goal in the first place, or that my goal was unrealistic.

By sharing with them when I'm not successful in attaining my goal, I can show them how I can learn from my mistakes when preparing to set a new goal.

The students will become more successful with this activity over time.

Around the third time through this process, I'm confident you'll start to see some pretty positive results.

## NAME STICKS IN A CUP

This strategy has been around forever, and for good reason—it's fair and it gets everyone involved! Ask each child to come up with a positive word that describes them, and which also has the same beginning sound as that of their first name. The word should be something with which they strongly identify, or which describes them in a positive way.

**Example:** Bright Bill, Jolly Joe and Awesome Andrea.

Put the names with their descriptor on a popsicle stick and place them in one of the many coffee mugs you receive as Christmas gifts each year.

Use the sticks to randomly call on students to read, answer questions, choose volunteers or any other time you need to choose someone fairly.

This method is not only fair, but it keeps everyone in the room involved. If the students know they could be called on without raising their hands, this encourages them to pay attention more closely. It also adds a certain element of fun to the classroom, because it's like having a little lottery drawing take place right in your own room.

# NUMBERS

**PURPOSE:** This is a game designed to be played as an ice-breaker to help everyone become more comfortable with each other. Numbers is great to play the first day of school or after a long break. This is a quick, easy game that can also be played as a reward for the team giving extra effort at the end of a long test, assembly or an extra hard day.

**TIME:** 5-10 minutes.

**SPACE:** You need enough space for the kids to walk around without bumping into anything. Ideally, this game is best played outside or in an open space like a project area, band room, or gym.

**SET-UP:**

> (This is a lot like "musical chairs" except there are no chairs and no music. Play up the fact that this is a game to help build trust in the group, and that everyone wins if no one gets hurt.)

1.  Instruct the kids to stand silently in the middle of the playing space.

2.  Tell them that when you say "Go!" they should walk around the space, making eye contact with each other without talking.

3.  You'll call out a number, and the kids will have to scramble to become a group representing the number you called by grabbing and holding on to each other.

**Example:** You call out the number "three." The kids must become a group of "three" by grabbing and holding onto each other.

4. Tell the kids that if they're unable to become a group of three because everyone else has already been snatched up, they must sit out until the next game.

5. Explain that one of the objects of the game is to be one of the last two people left in the game. They win the game.

6. Emphasize that the other objective of the game is to have fun while keeping each other safe. Make it clear to everyone playing the game that you will remove anyone from the game if they play too roughly and risk the safety of their teammates.

7. After you call a number, the kids get into groups representing that number, and the kids left over move out of the space, tell the kids to "move around" as they did before—eye contact and no talking.

8. Before you begin to play, tell the kids there are a few important rules and strategies they need to keep in mind:

   a. They cannot talk until you call a number.

   b. If the number "one" is called and they touch anyone else, they're out.

   c. They need to be ready to jump from one group to another if that action will match the number called.

   d. They must keep each other safe.

9. If you play this with a new group that doesn't really know each other, let them exchange names while they're in their group before calling another number.

**10.** If time permits, play more than once and encourage those who went out quickly to try to stay in the game longer each round.

**TEAM CONNECTION:** After the game you can target-talk about how important teamwork will be this year in order for them to have their best year ever.

Use this game to help show how working together was vital in order for them to be successful. Ask them how they see this carrying over into the classroom this year, and ask them to name some ways they can work together to make this their best year ever.

**FINAL THOUGHTS:** I want to thank Ms. Penny Owen, a former instructor of mine (and good friend) for introducing this game to me many years ago during a theater class she taught at Lansing Community College.

This activity has become a first day of school tradition in my room and is one of my students' favorite activities every year. They will often beg me to make room for this activity in our day. This makes a great incentive for them to work for. I've never seen any other activity break down walls so fast between strangers as this game—and that includes adults as well.

## NO TRASH TALK TOLERATED

Make it clear to your students that you will not tolerate any put-downs in your room—which also includes such favorites as "shut-up," "sucks," "crap" and "blows."

I'm amazed at how many times I hear kids telling each other to shut up as I walk down our hallways or when I'm outside at recess. Usually, it's said in a very negative, serious way.

I believe that when kids talk to each other in this fashion, it clearly shows a lack of respect for one another. It can tear down any sense of team you're trying to build in your room. Therefore, I will not tolerate any negative talk toward any teammate.

I dish out pretty severe penalties for put-downs in my classroom to help send the message that I won't put up with it. If I hear "shut-up" used by any of my students, I'll take away a recess for the whole class—even if it was said in a joking manner. I do this to help motivate the kids to remind each other not to do it. Nothing like a little positive peer pressure to help you out.

If a couple of students aren't getting along, I remind them that on our team we must all be able to work well together. I give them the opportunity to work their problems out for themselves, or they can sit out a few recesses together until they can develop, and show me a plan they'll be able to follow to help resolve any conflicts between them.

This may seem a tad strict, but when you walk into my room or spend some extended time with my kids, you can't help but notice that they treat each other well. I believe a lot of that has to do with the way we talk to one another.

It's your room. Expect the best out of your team and work with them to get it!

## 100TH DAY CELEBRATION

Celebrate the 100th day of school with your students, and use it as a midway check-up point to see how everyone (including yourself) is doing with regard to having their best year ever. Ask the kids to fill out an evaluation of the first 100 days, and write out specific goals for the remaining part of the year. The following is a "100th Day Celebration" form to use with your students.

---

## Best Year Ever!
## 100TH DAY CELEBRATION

◆ What's Your Favorite Memory of this Year So Far?

◆ What Are You Doing to Make this Your Best Year Ever?

◆ What's Your Favorite Coin Story So Far this Year?

◆ What Is Your Biggest Accomplishment So Far this Year?

◆ What Can You Do to Challenge Yourself to Make the Rest of this Year Truly Your Best Year Ever?

◆ What Can I Do to Challenge You to Be the Best You Can Be?

---

Bring treats for your students to show your appreciation for their hard work up to this point in the year and encourage them to finish the second part of the year just as strong—if not stronger.

The 100th day of school takes place in the dead of winter, usually somewhere between winter break and spring break. Everyone is looking for something to get excited about, so use this day to give your students something positive on which to focus. Start talking about the big event a few days prior to the date to help build anticipation and excitement in your room.

I tell my students that we've just gone over the half-way mark and that the second half of the year usually goes faster than the first half. I let them know how much I enjoy working with them as a team. I encourage them to take a few minutes to reflect on how nice it's been and to appreciate what we have, because, before we know it, we'll be disbanding the team for summer break.

This is usually the first time my students start thinking about the fact that what we've been working to build in our classroom this year isn't going to last forever. Therefore, we should take time to really appreciate it while we still have it.

I tell them we're working to make something very special that can't be taken away from us at the end of the year—our memories of the year. I remind them that we can always look back at this year as one of our best years ever if we continue to work now to make it happen.

Again, I'm planting a seed in their minds that what we have is very special, confident that they'll believe it and help to achieve it.

## ONE-ON-ONE IN ONE

This is an idea inspired by the book, *The One Minute Manager*.

When you need to discipline a child, talk with that child privately in the hallway outside the classroom. In a calm, quiet, serious tone—and in one minute (or less)—let that child know specifically what behavior or choice you're disappointed with, emphasize to them that you expect more out of them in the future, and remind them that you care about them and want to see them doing the right thing because it's the right thing to do. Always end your conversation in a positive way.

Keeping this to a minute (or less) doesn't allow time for the incident to turn personal, become a lecture or turn into a debate. It's short, to the point, and then it's over with so the child has a chance to get on with their day, ready to make the needed adjustments to have a good one.

Follow the same approach with praising. Keep it to a minute (or less), really making it clear to the child that you're pleased with their behavior/choices. Let them know they're helping to make the team strong, and that you'll continue to count on their leadership. This private pat on the back can do a lot to encourage them to repeat that behavior/choice.

I try to catch kids doing good things in the classroom and often praise them in front of their peers to help encourage other students to follow suit. However, sometimes it's more appropriate to let a student know you appreciate their efforts privately, especially if it concerns their work with another student who may struggle academically or socially in your room.

I also believe a private thank-you or pat on the back can sometimes carry more weight than a public acknowledgment, especially if it prevents embarrassing the student.

By creating this strategy to talk privately—and briefly—with your students about positive and negative issues, the other kids will have no definite way of knowing what you're talking about and can't just assume it's negative.

> **NOTE:** I try not to send a child out of the room for misbehaving unless I feel it's absolutely necessary. I'll usually wait for a break in the action when the kids are working as a group or individually, and take that time to tap a student on the shoulder and ask to see them in the hallway.

## OPEN MIKE/SHOW-AND-TELL SHARING EXPERIENCES

Allow kids the opportunity to share important things from home with the class—like a pet, collection, or award. It usually takes little time and means a lot to the kids. Set up a schedule with your students as to when, how often and for how long these sharing times will take place.

**NOTE:** Make a clear policy that pets can only come to your class on a scheduled basis. You don't want parents dropping in with pets at inappropriate times.

Set aside one day a month where kids can sign up to perform a special talent for the class like a song, dance, skit or magic trick. It will take only about twenty minutes of your day, but will do a lot to boost morale on your team.

**NOTE:** This is a great team-building activity, because many kids will want to perform with a partner or in a small group. The kids will usually rehearse together during recess time or at home.

This is a great activity to start after winter break to help get the kids through the winter. You can set this up so that your students have to work to earn this activity. Once the kids experience this activity, it should become very popular and one they want to earn on a regular basis.

## PARENT INVOLVEMENT

Send a "Parent Help Wanted" sheet home asking for parent volunteers to help you grade papers, do bulletin boards, help with record keeping, tutor and assist in special projects. You'll be amazed by how many parents are looking for an opportunity to get involved in their child's classroom.

*Story: One year, I had a parent come in once a week to help out with paperwork and copying materials. I have to admit that I was a little nervous having a parent come in so often and sit in the room while I was teaching. I think part of my fear was that I wasn't sure of her motives for wanting to come in, and I was a little worried that she'd be keeping score of all the things I didn't do well.*

*Just the opposite happened! She became a huge fan of my teaching and gained even more appreciation for what all teachers have to do to get their job done. She'd go out in the community and talk up what we do to other parents.*

*She enjoyed what she was doing in the room so much she started coming more than once a week, and started taking on more responsibilities. She became a big part of our team and helped me out very much.*

*I found it interesting that other teachers were constantly telling me how they wished they had a supportive parent like that. They were jealous of all the help this parent was obviously giving me, and, yet, they had not asked any of their students' parents if they would like to volunteer.*

*I think many of my peers were waiting for this potential gold mine to find them instead of digging a little for it. This has the potential to be a win-win-win situation because your students, their parents, and you can all benefit from this opportunity.*

*I wasn't surprised a year later when this parent's younger son was placed in my room. I had teachers begging me to request the older son to be placed in their room so they'd have the benefit of working with this parent.*

*Sure enough, this parent found time to volunteer in both her sons' rooms that year. Since that time, I've seen more parent volunteers in our building.*

## PRAISE/RECOGNITION/VALIDATION

Get in the habit of catching your students doing something "right" more often then catching them doing something "wrong." Take a second out of your day and praise them for their good work. Praise them in front of their peers—especially if you're hoping to motivate others to do the same.

**Example:** Whenever I see someone working on something where they're giving their best effort, I hold their work up and praise it to the class, telling them that's the type of effort I'm looking for.

Students will usually come up to show me what they have done when they're proud of something. Knowing they're feeling pretty good about their work, I'll praise it loudly enough for everyone to hear, or I'll hold it up for all to see.

Make sure the praise is sincere. Sincere praise will encourage them to repeat whatever you're praising. Kids want to be noticed. Why not notice them doing something well? They'll keep that in mind the next time they want to be noticed.

The same is true for validation. We all want to be validated. Be sure to take time to validate your students—let them know they're good kids and that they're capable of achieving whatever they set their minds to achieve.

If a kid hears this enough times from you—and really believes you believe it—they'll work extremely hard to live up to it. They don't want you to change this positive opinion you have of them.

*Story: One day, about midway through the year, I took our room's student council representative out in the hallway to talk about a minor concern I had about his not giving his usual effort during a lesson.*

*I was amazed when he started crying, telling me he was a bad kid. I told him I felt just the opposite about him, and that I felt he was putting too much pressure on himself to be perfect. He explained that in years past he had problems behaving in class, and believed his teachers saw him as a bad kid. He said he'd been working real hard this year to please me, because I told him earlier in the year that I thought he was a positive leader in our room.*

*He was worried that I was losing my strong opinion of him because of this one mistake. He didn't want me to look at him in the same way that he felt past teachers had looked at him. I told him to relax and just keep doing what he has been doing, and on the rare occasions when he made a mistake, to learn from it and try not to repeat it.*

*I ended our conversation by reminding him that I'm not looking for anyone to be perfect in our room. I told him to relax and keep on being the good kid that I know he is.*

*This boy continued to be a strong, positive leader in my classroom.*

## READ TO YOUR STUDENTS

Find some fun books and read to your students. You may want to read to them right after lunch to help them calm down for a productive afternoon. This is another time that kids can use wisely to work on homework assignments or on-going projects.

Choose books with interesting characters that you enjoy reading. Read them with lots of expression, and you'll have a captivated audience that will beg you not to stop and will look forward to your next reading session.

You can also choose books where the main character shows perseverance or gives extra effort to go after something he or she really wants. You can use target talk with the students to help emphasize character traits on which you want them to concentrate for themselves. Don't be surprised if your students start making these types of connections even before you do.

**Idea:** If you get a chance, read *There's a Boy in the Girls' Bathroom*, by Louis Sachar. This book is about a boy, Bradley Chaulkers, who goes from having a bad year—like every year—to having his best year ever.

This is a very funny book that will give you a lot to talk about with your students. I highly recommend it.

# REPETITION, REPETITION, REPETITION

The key to making this program work in your classroom and to see powerful results is repetition! You have to be willing to repeat the things you want your students to think about and do it over and over again—and then be willing to do it all over again!

Too many teachers will either tell their students what they want them to do once—and only once—or just assume their students should know what to do. That's a *huge* mistake! It will only set those teachers up for failure and a lot of frustration.

If you walk into your classroom the first day of school telling the kids they can have their best year ever, but don't do any follow-up, you won't be successful with this program. You must be willing to talk about what it will take for them to have their best year ever—every day—multiple times during each day, if possible.

The same is true if you want your students to start believing in their ability to control their own learning/future. You have to begin each day looking for ways to reinforce this type of positive thinking.

Your classroom behavior can stand out above the rest with a little repetition. Constantly remind your students what you're looking for and expecting them to do. It takes only seconds to do this, but can produce big results.

*Target talk* should be your number one tool to make this happen. Like a boxer, look for times to hit them with the powerful messages you want them to think about. Don't look for one knockout punch. Rather, think of your school year as a 15-round championship bout where you need to pace yourself and patiently wear down your opponents—negative thinking and bad habits—with a bunch of little punches.

The more you use target talk, the more you'll find times when you can effortlessly slip it into whatever you are doing. The more repetition you can use with your students, the better your chance of getting the results you want. Use repetition enough in your room, and you'll soon notice the kids using it themselves.

I believe this is so important, I'm going to repeat this whole thing one more time: **REPETITION, REPETITION, REPETITION**

Just kidding!

## REWARDS

Have you ever received a note from a parent or administrator telling you that they appreciate your efforts? If so, I'll bet you've kept it. I know I have. Why? Because it feels good to get that recognition from someone you're working for.

Many businesses—unfortunately education isn't usually one of them—give employees a chance to earn commissions or year-end bonuses. They use these to help motivate their employees to work harder and to keep up the good work.

Use little rewards or bonuses as incentives for your students to earn throughout the year. Stickers, treats, extra recesses, positive notes home to parents and other rewards can help motivate and inspire kids to do their best.

**NOTE:** I understand that kids should do the right thing because it's the right thing to do, and not just to get something. You definitely need to strike a balance when using a reward system, so that your rewards don't become "doggie treats" for your students to earn by jumping through hoops.

However, keep in mind how you feel when your work and extra effort isn't being recognized. Odds are that you'll keep performing at that level if you're being professional, but your morale will probably start to drop. How many teachers do you know who feel unappreciated for all their hard work?

The following are two rewards you can use to help recognize individual and team effort.

### Team Awards

Make up team-award certificates to reward the team with for doing something extra special as a group. This could be something as simple as getting a glowing sub-report that describes your group's excellent behavior while you were gone or out of the room.

Display these awards somewhere in the room as they accumulate them. Explain that you don't give these awards out often, so they should feel pretty good when they earn one. Challenge them to earn as many as they can throughout the year.

> **Idea:** Keep a record of how many awards your class earns and then challenge your next group to see if they can beat that record.

### Team Assist Awards

Make up a team-assist award certificate that you can give to individual students every so often to reward their extra effort or for doing something special for someone else on your team.

Put their name and the reason they're receiving the honor on the certificate. Use these on rare occasions to help keep their value high. Students who receive them will want to take them home to show their folks, and the other kids in your room will want to earn one for themselves.

> **Example:** I made a certificate that has a picture of a soccer ball and the words "Team-Assist Award" written at the top. At the bottom of the certificate is space for their name, date and what they did to earn the award.

I'll usually put their award on their desk so they'll see it first thing in the morning. It can really help to kick-start their day.

# RULES WORKSHOP

**OVERVIEW:** This is an activity designed to encourage your students to work together to help create five rules your class will adopt and follow for the year. Asking the kids to help create the rules will help to give them more ownership and should make them more accountable to their own rules. It's hard for a child to argue that a rule is unfair when they helped to create it.

**TIME:** This activity should be started the first day of school. The activity takes 60-90 minutes, depending on the amount of discussion time you want. I usually break this into three mini-sessions, each lasting about 30 minutes.

**MATERIALS:** lined paper, pencils, markers, chart paper and masking tape.

**SPACE:** A classroom setting where kids can work in small groups (at desks/on floor) and enough wall or board space to hang chart paper to display group work.

**SET-UP:**

**Session One:**

1.  Divide your class into groups of four and have them sitting together.

2.  Divide each group of four into pairs; give each pair a pencil and a piece of lined paper.

3.  Once everyone is settled, ask partners to brainstorm a list of rules they think would make a positive, safe, learning environment that would allow all students to have their best year ever.

4.  Tell them to pretend they're the teacher trying to create the best classroom for their students, and give them five minutes to write their list of rules on their paper.

    **NOTE:** To help keep the noise level down, tell them to talk very quietly so they don't give away any of their best rules to other groups. This would be a good place to model what a quiet work voice sounds like.

5.  During these five minutes, encourage the partners to get as many rules down as they can.

6.  After the five minutes have expired, give them another five minutes to trim their list down to only five rules. Their job is to take their list and trim it down and combine their rules to come up with a list of their best five rules.

7.  Next, after the partners come up with their best five rules, pair up the partners at each table and give them five minutes to compare their lists and add their rules together on the back side of their paper to create one list between them.

8.  Allow each group five minutes to take their new list and trim it down to five rules between them. Remind them that their table is working to possibly create the five rules the class will adopt as classroom rules for the year.

9.  Finally, give each group a piece of chart paper and have them write their five rules—large enough so that everyone in the room will be able to read their rules when you hang them up around the room. This usually takes 7-10 minutes.

    **NOTE:** Give each group member a different color marker and tell them they'll be responsible for writing down at least one rule, and they must be ready to read and explain that rule to their classmates when they share as a whole group. This is designed to get everyone involved and help keep everyone focused.

10. This is usually a good place to end session one. You want to tell the kids not to discuss their rules with any other group until they hang them up and introduce them to the rest of the class. Collect chart paper with the rules written on them along with the other materials.

   **NOTE:** I usually do this activity during the afternoon of the first day of school. I usually do the second session the following morning.

**Session Two:**

1. If the kids aren't already sitting with their group members, move them into their groups and pass out their chart paper from the previous lesson.

2. Give them five minutes to review their rules and remember which group member wrote which rule. Also, they need to practice reading their rule and how they're going to explain the rule to the group if asked by a classmate to clarify its meaning.

3. After the five minutes have passed, remind the class that today each group will get up and introduce the five rules they think the class should adopt to help ensure everyone a working environment that can help them have their best year ever.

4. Call up the first group and tape their piece of chart paper with the rules on it to the blackboard or wall, and ask each member (or partner) to read their rule—the one they wrote down—to the rest of the class.

5. When they've finished reading their rules, ask the rest of the class if they have any questions before you allow them

to sit down. Once all questions have been answered, lead the class in applauding their effort.

NOTE: It's important for the kids to show their appreciation for those who have taken risks by sharing in front of the class. I want every student in my room to feel that being in front of the class is a very comfortable place.

6. Ask the next group to come up and repeat steps 4-5. However, after they finish reading and explaining their rules—and before they sit down—ask the class to look at both groups' rules and see if they notice any similarities between them.

7. Take a marker and put a check next to any rules that are similar. The purpose is to start recognizing and highlighting those rules most often repeated.

NOTE: The more connections you and your class are able to make, the easier it will be to come up with five rules for the classroom that everyone can live with— and be able to claim ownership.

8. Repeat steps 6-7 until every group has had a chance to share and have their rules posted for everyone to see.

9. Finally, explain to the class that you'll take some time to look over all their rules and focus on those that have been identified as being repeated, and come up with a list of five rules that you hope will best represent their lists.

10. Leave their rules posted around the room until after you have introduced the class rules to the class. You can use them to point out how you developed your five rules from their lists. This will help them to buy into the rules sooner when it comes time to implement them.

**NOTE:** I usually use lunch time to decide on the five rules based on their lists. It doesn't take a lot of time to come up with the rules because they're usually pretty much the same year to year. I introduce the rules (third session) first thing after lunch on the second day of school.

**Session Three:**

1.  While the kids are at lunch, write your classroom's five rules on tag paper—one rule per piece.

2.  Thumbtack or tape the rules face down in the place where you will post the rules for the rest of the year. This builds suspense with the kids because they can't read them when they return from lunch until you're ready to unveil them.

    **NOTE:** I post our rules in the front of the classroom above the chalkboard. I explain to the kids that they're in that spot because they're essential for us to follow in order to have a safe, positive learning environment. By putting them in the front of the room, we'll be reminded often of what we each need to do to make our room special.

3.  Turn over (unveil) one rule at a time and read it to the class. Take time to thoroughly explain what that rule means, and model what the rule looks and sounds like. Then ask for and answer any questions pertaining to that rule before moving on.

4.  Show the kids how you came up with that rule based on their rules. Use their rules—still posted—to help build your case.

5.  Repeat steps 3-4 until you've explained all five rules.

6. After you introduce the class to the rules, this is a good time to explain the positive consequences for following the rules and the negative consequences for breaking the rules that you use in your room.

   **NOTE:** Following, are my classroom rules for this past year along with a quick explanation of the consequences that I use very consistently in my room.

## My Classroom Rules And Consequences

The following is an example of the rules my students helped to develop for our room.

**Classroom Rules:**

1. Listen to and follow all directions the first time.

2. Come to class with all materials, a positive attitude and give good effort. Be a positive team member.

3. Use good manners when others are talking. Raise your hand; be an active listener.

4. Treat other people, their belongings and school property with respect. Be kind.

5. Work during work periods, and use free time wisely. Complete and turn in assignments on time.

**Consequences:**

All names are kept in a notebook — not for public display.

Name Written Down = Warning/Reminder

✓ Name = Miss One-Half Recess

✓✓ Name = Miss Whole Recess

✓✓✓ Name = Parents Called In For Conference

## SIX STEPS TO SUCCESS

I'm fascinated by and want to know why some individuals and teams are able to succeed in doing extraordinary things while many others seem to just get by. It's become a hobby to read books dealing with personal growth, business management, leadership, motivation and psychology.

In all my readings, I began to notice that certain things were repeated over and over that seem to lead individuals/ teams to "success." Success can mean many different things to many different people. For our purpose, I'll define success as a positive feeling of accomplishment or feeling that you are living your life instead of just letting life live you—living with purpose!

The following is a summary of the six most common ingredients that seem to be needed for success to take place:

**1.** Believe You Can Achieve

**2.** Set Clear Goals

**3.** Take Action

**4.** Monitor And Adjust

**5.** Show Perseverance

**6.** Use Repetition

*Best Year Ever!* is designed to use these six steps with your students throughout the year to help them begin to form lifelong success habits that they can use to become more successful in their lives.

I want to take a moment and briefly describe each step, knowing that you'll get more understanding and ideas of how to include these into your classroom as you go through this activity section.

1. **BELIEVE YOU CAN ACHIEVE:** This seems to introduce any success story. It is the foundation on which everything else should be built. It is the belief one has that one can do something if one works for it.

   It is also positive thinking—being able to use your brain like a computer that you program. Like a garden, you learn to weed out the bad, self-defeating thoughts, and plant the positive thoughts you want to grow.

   Being able to visualize yourself already successful at whatever you want to succeed in seems to be a valuable skill many successful people have mastered.

2. **SET CLEAR GOALS:** It's the road map that leads to success. It's the target on which you set your sights and focus your energy.

   The key is to decide where you want to go, and then write down all the steps needed to get you there. Writing down your goals and looking at them often—checking your aim—seems to have more power than trying to remember them.

3. **TAKE ACTION:** This is the difference between wishing for something and making it happen! It's like when a little kid says, "I want to be a famous basketball player someday," yet never turns off the television long enough to practice.

   Once you set your goals and write them down, it is time to start working on them. For example, you can map out the most exciting vacation in the world, but unless you get in your car and drive out of your driveway, you won't get anywhere.

   Think of the process of taking action like learning to run. You first have to learn to crawl, walk and jog before you can run. Don't try to climb the mountain in one leap. Take action one step at a time, building momentum as you go.

4.  **MONITOR AND ADJUST:** This old classroom strategy also works in life. You have to be able to look up every once in a while and see whether you're still moving toward your target. If not, you have to be willing to change what you're doing to get back on track. You have to be willing to look at problems as opportunities to grow and mistakes as a chance to learn.

5.  **PERSEVERANCE:** This is where you have to adopt Thomas Edison's ability to stick with things long enough to get the results you want. Remember, it took him more than 10,000 tries to invent the light bulb.

6.  **REPETITION:** Redo steps one to five over-and-over again! This is the glue that will make it stick in your head and become a positive habit. Each of these steps will start to become second nature with enough practice and repetition.

*Best Year Ever!* is designed to help your students to start working on these six successful habits. Lead your students to consistently practice these six steps in as many different activities as possible to help them develop successful habits they can use for a lifetime.

## SUCCESS STORIES

**PURPOSE:** "Success Stories" is designed to inspire your students and give them plenty of real-life examples of how people have overcome setbacks in their lives or accomplished something special by dreaming big and then, working to make it happen, using at least one of the following:

◆  Setting clear goals

◆  Giving extra effort

◆ Maintaining a positive attitude

◆ Learning from mistakes

◆ Using perseverance

## Success Stories of the Rich And Famous

Find true stories about real people who were able to accomplish something special in their lives. This list should include famous athletes, business people, political leaders, civil rights leaders and entertainers—alive or dead.

Collect materials about these people and keep a record of where you can locate this material when needed.

NOTE: I use a monthly magazine called *Bits and Pieces* that specializes in telling such stories in a very brief format. Most stories can be read in less than two minutes. The bibliography at the back of this book lists this publication.

Read or show these stories to your students. Take five minutes afterward and ask the kids to name the principles on their coin that they feel the person used and mastered in order to become successful, and to explain their answer. Remind them that they have the same power within to make their dreams come true once they master and consistently use the principles on their coin.

NOTE: It's important to emphasize that these people were not born lucky or suddenly got lucky; rather, that they had to work hard and persevere to make their luck happen. You'll discover that, in many cases, the people you learn about came from less-than-ideal situations. It's important for the students to realize that they'll empower themselves so much more when *they* decide to make their luck happen—using the principles on their coin—than by waiting around for luck to find them.

These stories don't take much time, but when used consistently, over a period of time, can have a strong impact on your students.

## Success Stories From the People Next Door

Send letters to people in your community asking them to come into your room and share a story with your students about something special they've accomplished in their lives.

These don't have to be huge "Movie of the Week" or "stop the presses" stories. We've all done things in our lives that we're proud of, but many people will never know about them. However, these things would make excellent stories to help show young students that success is all around them, if only they apply the right principles.

**Example:** I tell my students the story about my high school soccer coach telling me he didn't think I was big enough or skilled enough to play college soccer. I was devastated, but quickly became determined to prove him wrong.

I spent many long hours lifting weights, running the streets of my town, and working on ball skills in the backyard. I had never worked so hard for anything in my life.

In the end, I lettered four years at Western Michigan University, was selected as a captain, and received a partial scholarship my senior season.

Even though this story will never be turned into a best seller, I'm proud of that accomplishment, and believe it can remind students that everyday people in their lives have experienced success by applying the principles on the coin to their lives.

You can ask parents, older students, other teachers and local celebrities to come to your room and talk to your kids for five to twenty minutes. You should video tape them, if possible, so you can build a "success story library" to share with other people in your school.

**NOTE:** From my experience, most parents love to be invited into their child's classroom. Involving parents in this activity will not only make them happy and make their child proud, but will also help make them even more supportive and appreciative of your efforts. This is a great win-win situation.

Invite a guest speaker once a month, or once a week if you get a lot of responses from your invitations. Be sure your letter makes clear the purpose of the story and types of stories you're looking for. This will help the speakers be more successful when talking to your group.

Remember to send a thank-you note as a follow-up to their visit. This can make a great activity for your students and will mean a lot to your guests.

**(Sample Letter to Parents Looking for Volunteers)**

---

### WANTED: SUCCESS STORIES

I'm looking for parents, older students and people from the community to volunteer fifteen minutes of their time to come in and share a story with my students about a personal success they've accomplished.

These don't have to be huge "Movie of the Week" or "stop the presses" stories. We've all done things in our lives we're proud of, that many people will never know about. These stories can give young students real-life examples of how people around them have applied certain strategies to overcome obstacles in their lives or worked to reach designated goals they set for themselves.

The story I shared with my students was how I was told by my high school coach that I would probably be unable to play collegiate soccer, but through hard work and perseverance, I ended up lettering four years at Western Michigan University and was selected as a captain and received a partial scholarship my senior season.

Even though this story will never be turned into a best seller, I'm proud of that accomplishment, and I believe it can remind students that if they have a burning desire to do something in their lives, believe they can do it, and are willing to work hard for it, they can make it happen!

There are many famous role models for children to study and emulate. However, if not done carefully, it's easy to give a message that only a few are able to reach their goals and do something special with their lives—meaning that only the famous people we see/read about are special enough or lucky enough to get what they want out of life.

---

By having local volunteers from all walks of life come in and share success stories from their own lives, we can work together to show our students that successful people are all around us—not just on television or in the news.

Also, if enough volunteers share their success stories, I believe that we'll be able to find similar principles or strategies being used by these people to help come up with a common success formula that we all can use.

If you would be willing to volunteer a little of your time for such a powerful cause, please fill out and return the form below. Your help on this project has the potential to guide these young students to believing that they have the power within to be a success in whatever endeavor they choose to pursue in life.

Thank you.

Mr. Cecil


Name:_____

Phone # :_____

Best time to call you to discuss this project:_____

Please check one of the following:

__ I have a personal story I would be willing to share.

__ I have a story I would like to share about a personal hero of mine or someone I admire for their accomplishment(s).

# TEAM CHALLENGES

Kids love little challenges throughout their day. It can be as simple as getting something cleaned up in a certain amount of time. Posed as a challenge, a chore suddenly becomes fun. Sometimes it's beneficial to make a big deal out of nothing.

Create larger challenges for the kids to work together to accomplish. Offer a small treat or prize to give some added incentive.

**Example:** This is a partial list of some of the challenges I have presented to my teams over the years.

◆ No one absent during the week = 10 minutes extra recess on Friday.

◆ No class checks on board during the week = gum day on Friday.

◆ The group's plant that looks the best after each term wins a piece of candy for each group member.

◆ The group that scores the best in a review game receives an automatic "A" on the final test—which they don't have to take.

◆ Kids who can beat their last year's attendance record—unless it was perfect attendance—get to enjoy a pizza party on me.

◆ Each year I challenge my kids to come up with better invention projects than my previous class.

◆ To break team records from the year before.

**Warning:** It's important to keep your challenges from becoming personal or hurtful. As much as my students like to compete against classes from previous years, I've discovered that they don't like to be compared to each other, especially in a negative way.

I have a teaching partner with whom I switch classes during the day. I've made the mistake of telling my group that I felt my teaching partner's class out-performed/behaved them on certain occasions. I'm sure you can imagine how my class reacted to that. It would be similar to a parent comparing you to another teacher and found you were coming up a little short.

## TEAM GOALS

Most people wouldn't think of starting a long car trip without having a clear destination in mind. The same is true with most winning teams. They don't start a season without a clear set of goals that everyone on the team is committed to work for.

However, this isn't usually the case with teachers and their students. Both may have goals, but not necessarily the same ones. The teacher may want to zip through the curriculum with the least amount of disruptions, while the students just want to survive each day long enough to enjoy another recess.

Seriously, how many classes do you know where the group has taken the time to establish a set of goals and have committed to achieving them?

My guess is not many.

How many classrooms have you walked into where the goals are clearly stated and posted for all to see?

My guess is even fewer—if any!

You have the opportunity to stand out in your school as a team that truly knows where it's headed. You can work with your group to establish a set of goals about which everyone is excited and committed to achieving. Once your team establishes its goals, post them in the room to serve as a constant reminder to everyone as to what you are all working to achieve.

**Example:** I post our goals on the wall opposite the door that leads into my room. I write the goals on bright yellow chart paper so they stand out to everyone entering our room. You can't walk into my room without noticing them.

You may want to wait a week or so to set your team goals. This gives the kids time to adjust to the new year and all that comes with it. I recommend following the same setup that was used in the "Rules Workshop" activity. Before you begin, you may first want to discuss how winning teams usually set goals at the beginning of their season, and how families usually determine what they want to do on their vacation before leaving their driveway.

## TEAM RECORDS

With all this talk about "team" in your room, don't be surprised if your kids want to compete against other groups to show that they're number one. I don't think this is a bad thing. They need to face some win/lose-type situations to see how they're doing compared to others.

Without this chance to compete, it will become hard for you to keep them functioning at a high level. How long would kids stay interested and continue to practice with intensity if they played on a soccer team that never had any games? Giving your students experiences that allow them to "go for the gold" will be essential if you want your team to stay interested in reaching their full potential.

Having said all that, you *don't* want your kids to walk around the school "trash talking" other students, "We're #1 and you're not!" It goes against the message that there is room at the top for every class to become the best they can be. So what can you do?

Team records are a great way to give your current students someone safe to compete against. Team records consist of little records that you keep year to year from the previous classes. Let your current students work together to try and beat those records. In a sense, your current students are competing against a team that no longer exists, but still seems very real to them.

**Example:** The following is a partial list of records I keep from one year to the next so my current team has something to shoot for:

◆ Most consecutive catches without a drop (see "Toss A Ball").

◆ Most team awards in one year (see "Rewards").

◆ Least amount of missed recesses for the whole class due to behavior concerns.

◆ Missed fewer days of school than last year's total.

◆ Total number of hallway compliments earned.

Team records work great if you mention the records enough for the kids to be able to set their sights on them. They get very excited when they're able to break a record by setting a new record for next year's team to shoot for.

## "TEAM" VS. "OUR CLASS"

One of the most common things I hear, when I ask kids what they really like about being in my classroom, is how I refer to us as being a team rather than just a class.

Target-talk that term often and see how your class responds.

## TOSS A BALL

Find a time in your room where kids are expected to raise their hands and answer questions. It could be for review questions after reading a story or reviewing a concept or chapter covered before a quiz or test.

Let the kids pass a ball around the room as they attempt to answer each question. Call on a child with their hand raised and have the child with the ball pass it to them to catch before they answer your question.

Keep track of the number of catches your class can make without a drop. Set a goal to beat that record, seeing how far you can go. Find a place in the room—such as a corner of your blackboard—where you can keep an on-going record of their day-to-day total and their highest total for the year.

**Idea:** At the end of the year, write down your class's record for consecutive catches, and let this become a record for your next year's team to aim for.

*Story: I use a soft football during our DOL* (Daily Oral Language) *exercise to help involve everyone while trying to inject a little fun into an exercise that can be pretty dry by itself. Kids are expected to make corrections on a sentence—full of errors—written on the board.*

*During the year we keep track of their team record, while trying to beat last year's record. One day, when all the planets must have been in perfect alignment, my team beat their record and was on the verge of beating the record set by the last year's group, which they had been trying to beat for seven months.*

*The excitement in the air was electrifying! I couldn't believe how badly they wanted this record. They knew this might be their last real chance of beating that team's record and they didn't want to come up short. I couldn't believe I was getting butterflies in my stomach rooting for them not to drop the ball.*

*If you were in my room that Thursday morning, I'm sure you would have been amazed at the level of intensity these kids were giving for an exercise we had done over a hundred times that year. When the record-breaking catch finally occurred, my students celebrated like they'd just won a state championship! They roared so loudly that I could hear other teachers shutting their doors.*

I'm truly amazed at how such a little event—like tossing a ball around the room—can bring such joy and enthusiasm into our day.

Make special rules to help keep this activity fun and safe for all involved. Tell the kids that if they have three dropped balls in one session, they'll lose the ball for a specified amount of time—like a week. This will help keep kids from getting too careless or silly with their throws.

Tell your students you will not use this activity if they can't keep each other safe. Again, this should help students avoid making bad choices. They'll feel a lot of positive peer pressure to keep this activity going in your room.

**Idea:** You can use your name sticks in a cup to decide which student attempts the next catch. This keeps everyone involved and can make for some interesting throws—some far and some close. You can also use the name sticks in a cup to decide who will be the counter for the day to help keep track of your students' catches.

## USE YOUR OFFICE SPARINGLY

Use your office only for major rules violations—like fighting, harassment, disrespect—to send a strong message to the kids that certain things will not be tolerated. This will create a win-win situation for your administrators and yourself.

Handling most discipline issues yourself helps to lighten the load for your administrators, which they will greatly appreciate and take note. This will send a clear message to your students that you are running the show and in control. You also get to deal with incidents to your liking.

## WIN-WIN SITUATION

Always look for ways where everyone on your team wins. Create a room where the kids clearly know that you're rooting for their success. Keep your high expectations and consistent discipline, but somewhere in there make sure your kids know you're working to help them have a winning year—their best year ever—and you can't lose!

Your students will respond to you in the most positive way if they truly believe you're working to create a winning situation for them. More than half your battles as a teacher are gone once your students are working just as hard to please you as you're working to please them.

Parents will also become your biggest allies when they have an enthusiastic child coming home each night, talking about their day in school, or about their whole year. You can't lose when you look for as many win-win situations as you can find during your **Best Year Ever!**

# APPENDIX TWO

# THIRTY DAY
# KICK-OFF
# PLANNER

# THIRTY DAY PLANNER

## INTRODUCTION

Have you ever attended a really interesting class or conference where you got a zillion really cool ideas you couldn't wait to take back and use in your classroom? Have you ever returned from such a conference or class, and a month later, realized you weren't consistently using any of those ideas on a regular basis?

That happens to me all the time!

I'm always looking for new and interesting ways to avoid getting bored or stuck in a rut with my teaching. Therefore, I'm constantly on the look-out for conferences that offer something different than what I'm already doing in my classroom.

Too often, I will come back from a conference re-energized and excited to try some new things in my classroom only to find out later I didn't really implement as many of those great ideas that I was so interested in discovering.

So, what's up with that? I liked the ideas, I was motivated to try them, and I had a pretty clear vision of how I thought they would improve my teaching. And yet, somewhere between the buzz of the conference and the hustle-bustle of my classroom, the ideas got lost!

Finally, I figured out what happens each time this occurs. It is called "life." That's it! Life gets in the way! We get back into our 100 m.p.h. classrooms, and it takes almost everything we have just to stay afloat. The new ideas get placed on the back burners to simmer while we work like mad to keep what's already in our pots from boiling over. Pretty soon we have so much on our stove that the new stuff falls to the wayside.

I don't want that to happen with my *Best Year Ever!* program you have just received!

Therefore, I have created this *Thirty Day Planner* to help you keep this on the front burners in your classroom. I want this to become the main course that you can consistently use to feed your students throughout the year.

Here is my plan! If you use *Best Year Ever!* a little each day—for thirty days—you'll use it the entire year. Like a good exercise program or diet, if you can stick with it long enough to start seeing results, you will have a better chance of sticking with it for the long haul.

I want you to commit to using *Best Year Ever!* in your classroom long enough to see the amazing results it has shown me in my own classroom—year after year. I also believe that by using it for thirty days, it will become a habit you'll use in your room the rest of the year.

I'm confident that your students won't let you stop using it after the first thirty days because, they'll be pleased with the learning environment that you have been working with them to create.

The second reason I've designed this *Thirty Day Planner* is to help get you over the hump of getting your new school year started. Beginning a new year is always exciting, but I believe it is also the hardest part of the year!

With all the time and energy it takes to get your room up and running, it doesn't leave you with a lot of left over time to deal with implementing a new program. Therefore, I've done much of the work and planning for you by providing you with quick, easy lesson plans to follow along with Section Two of this book *(Best Year Ever! A Year Long Theme That Focuses on Team)*.

I'm confident that if you consistently use this planner for the next thirty days, you'll see amazing results beginning to take place on your team. You'll have created a caring community of individuals working together to enable everyone to reach their personal best.

If you ever have any questions, please know that you can call **(800-690-1233)** or e-mail me **(BillCecil@BestYearEver.net)**. I will get back with you—usually within a day or two.

Finally, remember to have fun with this! Follow the plans exactly as written or change them to better fit your needs or the needs of your team. The main thing is to try and stick with this approach for at least thirty days—long enough to start seeing powerful results.

# DAY ONE

## Idea: Count Up the Days

1. Find a corner of your chalkboard where you can keep track of the number of days you have in your *Best Year Ever!* (B.Y.E!)

2. Write "B.Y.E! DAY" in that spot and draw a little box around it—leaving enough room to write the number of the day below it.

3. Write the number "1" in the box to represent this being the first day of your *Best Year Ever!*

    If your custodians wash your boards every night, *be sure to ask them not to erase this during the year.*

4. Each morning erase yesterday's number, and write today's new number in that space. I've made this a part of my morning ritual. Before my students arrive, I write up the day's agenda, the Quote of the Day, the Brain Warm-up, and the new number that represents the day we are on.

## Activity #1

*The Kick-Off*

1. Review pages 85-107, highlighting the main points you want to cover with your students.

2.    Write the "Quote of the Day" on the board with the following quote below it: "Your past doesn't equal your future!"

3.    Make sure you have a B.Y.E! coin in your pocket or on your desk that you can pass around to your students when you get to that part of the activity.

4.    Get a note card and write down a few notes or an outline of the different points you want to cover in your opening speech to the students. I usually write down the following notes to serve as a reminder of what I want to be sure to cover:

### *B.Y.E! NOTES*

- ☑ Attendance
- ☑ Attitude #1:  Positive Attitude
- ☑ Attitude #2:  Believe You Can Achieve
- ☑ Effort
- ☑ The Coin
- ☑ Coin Proposition
- ☑ I Care
- ☑ New Beginnings

**REMINDER:** Don't forget to mail home your "Parent Brochure" today so your students will receive them in the mail tomorrow to show their parents.

## Activity #2

### *Rules Workshop (Session One)*

1.    Review pages 204-206, highlighting the main points you want to cover with your students.

2.  Only cover "Session One" with your students the first day of school. I usually wait to do this activity in the afternoon, immediately following their lunch break.

3.  Make sure you have the materials listed on page 204 ready to go.

4.  Observe and write notes in your activity book that might help better prepare you for next year. I usually write down notes about the amount of time I allowed the students to work on each part—noting if it was too much or too little.

## Activity #3

*Numbers*

1.  This is a great activity to end your first day together.

2.  Review pages 190-192, highlighting the main points you want to cover with your students.

3.  This is a great game to play outside early in the school year. If it's hot outside, find a nice shady spot to play. Our school doesn't have air conditioning, so I use this game as a valid reason to get us outside—especially at the end of a long day.

4.  You may want to explain the game inside before going out to play, so your students are able to focus more on the rules of the game. Also, let them know that if they're able to stay focused on the game outside you'll be willing to play it a few times, but if they struggle to stay focused, you'll stop the game and bring everyone in.

5.  Make sure you follow the game with a discussion using the "Team Connection" from the lesson plans.

# DAY TWO

## Activity #1

*Getting Their Commitment*

1. Review pages 108-115, highlighting the main points you want to cover with your students.

2. Remind your students that they'll have the entire school day to decide whether they're willing to commit to working on their attendance, attitude, and effort for the whole year. Tell them you'll pass out the coins at the end of the day.

3. Make sure that each child who takes a coin from you realizes they're making a promise to you to work to have their B.Y.E! I ask them to look me in the eyes and tell me they will work to have their B.Y.E!

## Activity #2

*Rules Workshop (Sessions Two and Three)*

1. Review pages 206-209, highlighting the main points you want to cover with your students.

2. I recommend doing "Session Two" before lunch and "Session Three" after lunch.

3. Once you post the rules and go over each one with your students, ask them to raise their hands if they think any of the rules seem unfair or unrealistic to follow. Talk over any objections, and make needed changes if necessary until everyone is in agreement that these are now the class rules.

4. Explain the positive consequences for following the rules and the negative consequences for breaking the rules in your room.

5. Finish this activity by telling your students that the rules are now in place and that everyone is expected to follow them from this point on.

6.    Get a notebook to record names of students that have broken one of the posted rules. To save time, write the child's name and the number of the rule for which they needed a reminder.

7.    Be sure to start fresh each day by turning the page of the notebook or writing a new date down on the page.

**NOTE:** The ONLY way your rules will work is if you ENFORCE THEM CONSISTENTLY! You must enforce your rules every moment of every day in your room if you want to create a caring community in which your students can work to have their best year ever. I CANNOT STRESS THIS ENOUGH!

Therefore, don't hesitate to write a child's name down if they need a reminder to follow the rules. It sends a message—*especially early on in the year*—that you run a tight ship and have high expectations. The names you record the first few weeks of school—and there will be more early than later—will pave the way to having very few names on your pad the rest of the year. Your students will test you early and often until they know the limits! BE KIND, BE STRONG, AND BE CONSISTENT!

## Idea

*Seating Charts*

On the first day of school, I usually let my students come in and sit where they want. However, I move them on the second day into arranged seats. I try to mix the room up so that boys and girls are sitting together and are from different rooms or schools. I try to avoid "buddies" sitting next to each other to encourage everyone to start making friends with everyone in the class.

*See "Expectations For Working Relationships" on page 133.

# DAY THREE

## Idea

### Unofficial/Official Daily Greetings

1.  When the bell rings each morning, try to position yourself in the hallway, by your classroom door, so you can greet your students individually as they come in.

2.  Let them know you're glad to see them and that it's going to be a great day even before they have a chance to walk into your classroom.

3.  Don't be surprised, at first, if they don't give you much eye contact or seem overly eager to make small talk. This is probably a new experience for them—one that may take a little time for them to get comfortable with.

4.  When you're ready to get started with your day, walk into the classroom and say, "Good morning everyone, and welcome to day three of your *Best Year Ever!* Hopefully, you're working on your attendance, attitude and effort to help make it happen!" Starting off each morning this way will help reset the team/individual goals for the year every day.

5.  Don't be afraid to vary your official greeting slightly some mornings to help target-talk a particular point. For example, I may come in on a morning after a rough day and say to the class, "Good morning, everyone, and welcome to day 16 of your B.Y.E! I'm excited to see how well this team will rebound from yesterday by having a great day today."

    **NOTE:** Remember to change the B.Y.E! day count each morning on your chalkboard.

## Activity

### Partner Interviews

1.  Have each student interview another student in your classroom. You may want to pair up students according to

who they sit by in class or with someone they do not know. (Note: Review "Learning Partners" on pages 132-133.)

2. Give each student a sheet with specific questions you want them to ask each other—leaving room between each question for them to record their partner's answers. (See sample questions at the end of this section.)

3. Before they start their interviews, explain how you want them to conduct the interviews. For example, you may ask one student in each group to ask all their questions first while the other partner concentrates only on answering the questions, or you may have them take turns (alternating asking and answering questions) until all the questions are covered.

4. Tell the class they'll need to pay close attention to what their partner says and take good notes because, they'll be introducing their partner to the rest of the class in part two of this activity.

5. If they complete their interviews early, encourage them to make up a few additional interesting questions on the back of their sheet. Continue the interview procedure.

6. Part two of this activity is where you call up one pair of students at a time and have them introduce their partners to the rest of the class.

7. If possible, provide a chair for the person being introduced and have the person introducing them stand behind or next to them.

8. Encourage the students to try to avoid reading their notes— instead, have them try to use their notes as a reference only.

9. I wouldn't try to get through all of these in one session. Spread them out over a few days—doing a couple in the morning, between subjects, and a couple more in the afternoon, the same way. This will keep each interview presentation fresh and more interesting.

10.   Try to find one thing in each interview you can comment on or ask a question about to model your active listening skills and interest in wanting to know more about each of your students.

### SAMPLE INTERVIEW QUESTIONS

◆   What do your parents do for a living?

◆   How many brothers and sisters do you have?

◆   What kind of pets do you have, and what are their names?

◆   When you're not in school, what are some of your favorite things to do?

◆   What's the most exciting thing that's ever happened to you?

◆   If you won $1,000, what would you do with the money?

◆   What's one thing you want the rest of the class to know about you?

# DAY FOUR

## Activities #'s 1-3

### Brain Warm-Up Activities

1.   Reread the overview on page 162.

2.   Be sure to provide each student with a notebook so they can write down the Brain Warm-up Activities each day as part of their morning ritual.  This notebook can be used for your students to record their goals, daily assignments, quotes, things they are excited or happy about, puzzles, and other important information.

## Activity #1

*Name Three*

1.  Review pages 163-165, highlighting the main points you want to cover with your students.

2.  Come in with three things you're excited or happy about that you can share with your students. Do this each morning to help model to your students to look for things in their own lives that they are happy or excited about. Also, this is a great way to let your students learn more about you.

3.  Make it a part of your daily agenda. I write it on my board as part of the Brain Warm-up. "Brain Warm-up (+3)" is the first thing I write on my agenda each morning.

4.  Ask your students to write down their three choices and to share them with the student sitting next to them or with members in their group.

## Activity #2

*Brain Warm-Up Puzzle*

1.  Review pages 165-167, highlighting the main points you want to cover with your students.

2.  Start a file or collection of puzzles you can write on your board each day. Many teachers will have a collection of puzzles they'd probably share with you, so don't be shy about asking around your building. You can usually find puzzles in your newspapers, library, bookstores and on the Internet.

3.  Encourage students to write the Brain Warm-up Puzzles down, and try them out on family members at home. I don't force my students to write these down, but many will anyway.

4.  Develop a fair way to call on students to answer the puzzle when you're ready for them to answer it. I have each child's name on a popsicle stick that I randomly pull out of a coffee mug until someone gets the correct answer.

5.    If a puzzle is pretty difficult, leave it up on your board for a few days and offer a small treat to the first student that can answer it correctly and show the class how they came up with the answer.

## Activity #3

*Quote Of The Day*

1.    Review pages 167-169, highlighting the main points you want to cover with your students.

2.    Find a place on your chalkboard to write the "Quote of the Day" each morning. I put my quotes right next to my agenda each day.

3.    Choose a quote from the back of this planner to use, or choose your own. The quotes in the back of this planner are categorized by topic. Choose quotes that you think will be good for your class to talk about and focus on throughout the day. (See *Appendix 3*.)

4.    Ask your students to write these down each day, and then, show them to a "checker" in their group. This is a great way to make sure they're building their own collection of positive quotes.

# DAY FIVE

## Activity

*Teach, Model, Practice And Praise Procedures*

1.    Take some time to identify important daily procedures you want your students to master to help keep things running smoothly.  This provides you with more time and energy to teach.

2.    Here is a sample list of procedures you may want your students to master within the first month of school:

## CLASSROOM AND SCHOOL PROCEDURES

◆ Lining Up

◆ Walking in the Hallway

◆ Recess

◆ Fire Drills and Tornado Drills

◆ Work Time

◆ Free Time

◆ Sharpening Pencils

◆ Turning in Notes, Assignments, and Forms

◆ Cleaning the Room Before Leaving Each Day

◆ Watering Plants

◆ Passing Out Papers

◆ Asking Questions

◆ Working With Others

◆ Solving Problems

1.  Invest the time early in the year to teach a few different procedures each day or to review a procedure already taught.

2.  Don't assume your students will come to you at the beginning of the year with these procedures mastered, and don't waste your energy getting upset trying to understand why they don't already have them mastered.

3.  Teach them and practice them like you do fire drills.

4.  Every chance you get, model the way you expect them to follow each procedure.

5.  Consistently remind them before each procedure what you expect to see.

6.  Consistently praise them for following procedures, and, when possible, praise them in front of other students, staff members, and guests.

7.      Take some time and review pages 56-65.

**NOTE:** This is one area where your team can stand out in the building as being a special group. I invest a little time each day on this and it consistently yields high returns in terms of lower stress, more time to teach, and the enjoyment of working in an ongoing friendly, orderly climate.

# DAY SIX

## Activity

### *Goodbyes With Lots Of High Fives*

1.      Review pages 182-184, highlighting any main points you want to use with your class.

2.      When you drop your class off for a special activity like gym or music, stick your hand out as you say goodbye to them. Don't be surprised if they start "giving you five" as they walk by. Sometimes I will just be pointing at which side of the hallway I want my students to walk on, and they'll start lightly slapping my hand.

3.      Do the same thing at the end of the day as they're walking out the door. It's a great way to stay connected with your students. As they walk out the door, many of my students will wish me a nice night or weekend.

4.      Look around your building. Check to see how many staff members are making this type of a connection with their classes. You'll not only send a strong message to your students, but you'll also let other staff members see that you truly are working to stay connected with your team.

5.      Your students will start to really believe that you're their biggest fan, like you told them the first day of school. Many of them will work harder for you, because they'll really know you care about them.

# DAY SEVEN

## Activity

### *Team Vs. Our Class*

1.  Review pages 9-11and 116-117, highlighting the main points you want to cover with your class.

2.  Ask your students to share some examples of winning teams they've been a part of or have followed as a fan.

    **NOTE:** Don't limit your examples only to sports teams. Some may be involved in dance, theater and other non-athletic groups that would fit into this discussion.

3.  Share your own list of winning teams, and have a group discussion about what makes these teams fun to root for, play for or be a member of.

4.  Discuss the differences between a team and a family.

5.  Define what makes a group of individuals a team and the advantages they can enjoy by forming a team.

6.  Share the example from "Diversity = Strong Team" on pages 177-178, and take time with your students to find and identify examples of diversity in your room. Discuss ways that can make your team stronger.

7.  Finally, create a clear vision for your class that will allow them to see themselves becoming a winning team this year by taking advantage of the opportunities they have to work together to create something special.

    **NOTE #1:** Make a point to use "our team" instead of "our class" as often as possible. Try to target talk the word "team" into your teaching at least 3-4 times each day this week. When you start hearing them use this term, you'll know your team is starting to take shape. Don't expect them to grasp this concept overnight. Be patient!

NOTE #2: On "Day Thirteen" you'll be asked to do an activity with your class called "Identify Our Identities." In order for this to be successful, you'll need some old magazines that your students can cut pictures from. If you don't have any, make an offer to your students that you will give them a small treat (like a small piece of candy) if they bring in some old magazines that their parents have given them permission to donate to your classroom for this project. Write it somewhere on your board to serve as a daily reminder.

You definitely want to go through every magazine to make sure everything is appropriate to your standards.

# DAY EIGHT

## Activity

### Team Goals

1.   Review pages 219-220, highlighting any main points you want to cover with your students.

2.   You may want to take a few minutes to highlight some of the main points from your discussion about winning teams—focusing on how they all set clear team goals.

3.   Be sure to follow the "Rules Workshop" activity (pages 204-209) to help you set up this activity.

NOTE: You may want to help get them started by sharing some goals other teams working with *Best Year Ever!* have created. Below is a partial list of some of the goals my teams have come up with over the years:

### Sample Team Goals

◆  To have our B.Y.E!—or at least have fun trying!

◆  To challenge each other to try new things!

◆  Work to always give our best effort.

◆ Have the best attendance record in school.

◆ To make new friends and work to get along.

# DAY NINE

## Idea

### Team Challenges

1.   Review pages 218-219 about team challenges and start thinking of ways you can challenge your group that will require them to work as a team to be successful.

## Idea

### Team Awards

1.   Review pages 202-204, highlighting any ideas you want to use with your students.

2.   Find something in the next few days to give them a team award.

   **Example:** You may want to give them a team award for getting a compliment from another staff member about their behavior in the hallway.

3.   Make a big deal about how they worked as a team to earn that award and how proud you are of them for that.

4.   Find a place in the room to post their award.

5.   In the future, use a team award as something they can earn to help motivate them to give their best effort as a team.

   **NOTE:** The class will want to earn more of these awards if you make a big deal out of the first one or two they earn. I'm still amazed how a piece of paper hanging in the room becomes such a large motivation for the group to work as a team.

# DAY TEN

## Activity

*Name Sticks In A Cup*

1.     Review pages 189-190.

2.     You may want to mention to your students, first thing in the morning, that after lunch you'll be asking them to give you the positive descriptor that will go in front of their name on the stick.

3.     Encourage them to come up with a couple choices in case someone else chooses one of their choices.

4.     Tell them you'll provide them with a descriptor if they're unable to come up with a positive word on their own.

5.     Start using the cup as often as possible to keep everyone in your room involved.

# DAY ELEVEN

## Idea

*Cash In With Coin Connections*

1.     Take a few minutes to review pages 173-177, highlighting any ideas you want to use in your classroom.

2.     Challenge yourself to find as many different ways to make connections with the coin throughout each day.

3.     Try to get in the habit of holding the coin when you're trying to motivate your students to give their best effort on an assignment or some kind of group activity.

**Example:** I'll often walk around the room while they're working individually or in small groups on an assignment or project. I'll hold the coin as I walk around. It serves as a silent reminder to my students what my expectations are in our room.

## Activity

### Coin Connection #1

1.  Tell your students that every so often you will randomly call on someone to show their coin by choosing a name stick from the cup.

2.  If they can show you their coin, they will have earned the class a special small treat from you.

3.  Inform them that today's treat will be ten extra minutes of recess.

4.  Call on a student to show you their coin. You may need to let them get it out of their desk, folder or locker.

5.  When they show the coin, be sure to have the class thank them for giving them this treat. If the child does not have their coin, remind the class that they will still have their regular recess, and remind them how important it is to keep their coin handy because, you may do this again soon.

**NOTE:** I usually choose a student randomly to show me their coin. However, on special occasions I may choose a certain child who needs a pick-me-up or the chance to win points with their peers. This can do a lot to pick up a student's morale. Obviously, I try to make sure they have their coin before doing this.

# DAY TWELVE

## Idea #1

### Checkers Or Team Captains

1.  Choose a "team captain" or "checker" for each group of students who will help during the week to make sure the students in their group have their work completed, gather materials for the group, and collect and turn in any assignments when due.

**Example:** Each day in my classroom, I have my students write down three things they're excited or happy about, and copy the quote on the board into their agenda books. Instead of me walking around checking to make sure everyone does this each day, I assign the checkers or captains in each group to do this for me. They come to me if someone is not doing it, so I can work with that student in private later when I have a minute.

2.     Each week, choose a new person in the group to take on that role. One idea is to have the person next (clockwise) to last week's checker go next.

3.     Take a little time each week to remind the captains or checkers of their job responsibilities and how important it is that you can trust them to give this their best effort and to be honest.

## Idea #2

*Job Folder*

1.     Make a list of daily/weekly jobs that need to be completed in your room by students. Below is a partial list of some of the jobs I had listed in the folder:

   **a)** Take Down Attendance and Lunch Count

   **b)** Pass Out Any Notes or Papers At 2:20 P.M.

   **c)**  Help To Take Care Of Class Pet

   **d)** Water Certain Plants

   **e)** Erase Boards At 2:20 P.M.

2.     Laminate that list and place it inside a job folder marked "Job Folder." Go over each job inside the folder, explaining and modeling how you expect to see each job completed.

3.  Tell your students that each week you'll pass the folder to a new group, and it will be their responsibilities to make sure each job gets done.

    **NOTE:** You can let them decide who will do each job, or you can assign the captain or checker in the group to assign the jobs. I usually let the kids work that out for themselves, reminding them it's important for everyone to get a chance to do every job, if interested.

4.  Give the job folder to a new group each Monday morning.

# DAY THIRTEEN

## Activity

### *Identify Our Identities*

1.  Go over the information from "Diversity = Strong Team" on pages 177-178 with your students as an introduction to this activity.

2.  Read and follow the steps listed in "Identify Our Identities" on pages 184-186.

3.  Allow three or four sessions (30-40 minutes each) to finish this project.

4.  Each day when it comes time to clean up, give the class a five minute deadline to get the job done—which includes putting all materials away neatly, magazines returned and neatly stacked, and all scraps off the floor. You may want to use your team captains or checkers to help be in charge of organizing each group's efforts.

This is a great activity to have them work on the last part of the day—especially if the weather is hot outside. You may want to tell them that they cannot start gluing any pictures down until they have a checker make sure it completely covers the paper they'll be using. Encourage them to cut out big pictures because they'll have an easier time trying to cover their paper. Little pictures take forever, but they're good as fillers in the end.

Also, when someone gets done with their collage, assign them to work with a slower worker to help them get done faster. Make sure you only allow the students to cut out pictures that represent them in a positive way.

**NOTE:** My son's first grade teacher did a similar activity where she gave each child a puzzle piece that they would eventually put together to complete a wall puzzle. You could give each student a puzzle piece to cover with their pictures and then connect them to make the phrase "OUR TEAM" or "WINNING TEAM."

## DAY FOURTEEN

### Activity

*Behavior Reports*

1.  Review pages 152-153 and follow the steps as you prepare to send home the first behavior reports.

2.  There is a blank copy of the behavior report I use on page 154, and a sample of how I fill out my behavior reports on page 155.

3.  Remember to always start with the positives before reporting the things the students need to work on.

4.  At the beginning of the school year, I send this report home twice within the first thirty days of school and then at the end of each month the rest of the year.

5.  Make sure everyone's reports are signed by their parents and brought back by a certain date. I tell my students that the due date will be their ticket to recess that day.

**NOTE:** The first time you send these home is very important because it will show your students that they're truly being held accountable for their actions. Don't sugar-coat these reports in any way, and don't be discouraged if you send home a lot of reports with "Rules To Continue Working On" marked up. Send a message to your students that even though you may not yell and scream to get them to follow the rules, you still have very high expectations of them. Also, really play up the students who got a star at the top of their report. Give them their small treat in front of the others so they can see what they can earn. I give a Fireball or Jolly Rancher to students with perfect reports. I remind all the students that I'll send another report home in fifteen days, and that they can all start working tomorrow to earn a "starred" report.

# DAY FIFTEEN

### First Fifteen Days Check Point

You've reached day fifteen of your *Best Year Ever!* Hopefully, you've committed yourself to stick with the program and are starting to see results in your classroom. I hope you're beginning to feel that *Best Year Ever!* is taking root in your classroom and beginning to grow.

Remember, I believe the first thirty days are the most demanding days of your entire year. This is where you're setting the table for a successful rest of the year in your room. You're creating a caring community that will thrive once it is established.

Looking back over your first fifteen days, I hope the following items are a daily fixture in your classroom. If so, I know that *Best Year Ever!* will be in full bloom by the time you reach your thirtieth day.

## Best Year Ever!

### *Daily Fixtures In Your Classroom*

1.   Counting days and keeping track of them on the blackboard. (Day One)

2.   Rules are established and consistently enforced. (Day Two)

3.   You are there to greet your students at the door each morning. (Day Three)

4.   Start each morning by saying, "Welcome to day __ of your *Best Year Ever!* Hopefully, you're still working on your attendance, attitude and effort to help make it happen." (Day Three)

5.   Each student knows they have a learning partner to lean on and are responsible for each day. (Day Three)

6.   Each day includes Brain Warm-Up activities which includes the "Quote of the Day" and "Name Three." (Day Four)

7.   Taking time each day to say good-bye with lots of high fives. (Day Six)

8.   Using word "team" instead of "class" whenever possible. (Day Seven)

9.   Keeping everyone involved by using name sticks in a cup. (Day Eleven)

10.  Consistently using the coin to make connections to *Best Year Ever!* (Day Eleven)

11.  Using team captains or checkers and a job folder to help keep the room running smoothly. (Day Twelve)

It's exciting to think that in fifteen days you've already established so much of this program in your classroom. The next fifteen days won't be as time-demanding, so you can start working more on the curriculum you must teach this year.

The next fifteen days of this planner will take little time each day, but will play a huge role in further establishing a *Best Year Ever!* learning environment in your room. Think of using *Best Year Ever!* as a preventative maintenance program that will keep your team running smoothly as you work through the year.

# DAY SIXTEEN

## Activity

### S.S.O.T.W. (Success Skill Of The Week)

1.  Review pages 119-120 (Second Example), for a brief overview of this activity.

2.  Create a list of skills you'd like to focus on with your students throughout the year that will help to make them more successful in their lives.

### Sample Success Skills

| | |
|---|---|
| Attendance | Taking Action |
| Attitude | Perseverance |
| Effort | Humor |
| Belief in self | Curiosity |
| Visualize Success | Problem Solving |
| Goal Setting | Cooperation |

1.  Choose one skill at a time to focus on for a week or two in your classroom.

2.  Introduce the new skill by defining it and then providing plenty of examples of what that skill would look like (and sound like) if someone were using that skill.

3.  Find different ways to focus on that success skill during the next couple of weeks.

**Examples:** Read short stories of famous people using that skill, tell stories from your own life that reinforce the skill, and target talk (pages 118-121), the skill into your lessons as much as possible.

4.   Reward students you catch modeling or using the skill.

In my classroom, I choose a success skill every two weeks—usually on a Monday. I usually write the skill at the top of a piece of chart paper and under the skill draw a line down the paper dividing the paper into two columns.

At the top of one column, I write "Looks like . . ." and have the class discuss in their groups what this skill would look like if someone came into our room and saw them using the skill. They would only be able to rely on their sight because they would be deaf. After they discuss it in their small groups, we share and record responses on the chart paper as a large group.

I will then write, "Sounds like . . ." at the top of the second column and repeat the steps described above.

Other weeks, I might write "In the Classroom" and "In the Real World" and have the class discuss how these would apply in the classroom and in their home life or anywhere else outside of school—like sports teams, at work or around their neighborhood.

# DAY SEVENTEEN

## Activity

### Keep Room Professional Looking

1.   Review pages 123-124, "Professional Looking."

2.   Explain and show to your students how you'd like the room to look every time they leave as a group for recess, lunch, music or P.E.

3.  Don't allow them to drape sweaters or sweatshirts over the backs of their chairs.

4.  Ask them to keep their work area clean.

5.  Allow time at the beginning or end of each week to tidy up their desks.

6.  Conduct surprise desk inspections—complete with rewards and punishments.

7.  Work to keep your own work areas clean to help model your expectations to the students.

8.  Make sure they put chairs up and sweep each night before leaving to go home. Remind them it isn't the custodians' job to pick up after the mess they've made, but to keep the school clean and in working condition.

    NOTE: Sometimes little things make big differences! The way you keep your room looking makes big statements to your students and guests when they enter your room. Teach them to respect their work space because it will help them respect the work they do in that space—which will increase their overall pride.

# DAY EIGHTEEN

## Activity

*Six Steps To Success*

1.  Review pages 210-212, highlighting any of the main points you want to cover with your students.

2.  Go over this success formula with your students using examples from your own life or someone a little more famous (Thomas Edison, for example) to help make each step more clear.

3.     Ask them to share experiences in their lives where they have used this formula—maybe without even knowing it—to accomplish something important.

4.     Tell the class that they'll be using this formula often this year, to accomplish individual and team goals.

5.     Find ways to work this formula into your lessons—especially class projects—to help them become more comfortable using it.

6.     Find and read news articles and books of people who have used this formula successfully in their lives.

# DAY NINETEEN

## Activity

### Mini-Goals

1.     Carefully review and follow the steps listed on pages 187-189 with your students.

2.     Go over the steps from "Six Steps To Success" with your students, focusing on the first two steps.

3.     Really stress how important it is for them to choose a goal they want to work towards during the next month, and not one they think will impress others.

4.     Also, make it clear to them that they will not be graded on the outcome of making or missing this goal.

5.     Find time each day for the class to silently read and think about their goal.

6.     Be sure to set your own goal and share it with them. This is a great way to model this activity.

**NOTE:** Don't underestimate this activity! I attribute finishing writing this book to following and modeling this one.

# DAY TWENTY

## Activity

*The 'I Can' Pledge*

Some of my best ideas have come from other teachers using *Best Year Ever!* and sharing with me the new ways to teach and motivate that they've discovered while using this program. A good example comes from Denise Kehren, a 6th grade teacher in my school. She took an idea I mentioned on page 126 and created the "I Can" pledge written below. She has it posted on a wall in her room for kids to recite once a week.

### I CAN

I can choose to be happy.

I can choose to see the world as a world
of good and opportunity.

I can create the world I want to see.

I can be as smart as I choose to be.

I can have a good attendance record.

I can give effort consistently.

I can make mistakes and grow from them.

I can set and achieve goals this year.

I can focus on what I want to become or do.

I can tackle my "cannots."

I can have my **Best Year Ever!**

I CAN MAKE IT HAPPEN!

This year I'm going to have my students say the "Pledge of Allegiance" first thing each morning, and then the "I CAN" pledge.

What a great way to get them feeling in control of their learning each morning!

# DAY TWENTY-ONE

## Idea

*Take Away One Recess*

This is probably the most controversial thing I'm going to ask you to do when using this program. It's not popular with the students, and it is not popular with some parents, but it's important to do once early in the year, to let your students know you mean business.

I'm *not* asking you to pick a date on the calendar and decide that will be the day you'll take a recess away from your class. However, I *am* asking you to find a day sometime early in the year where they are not giving their best effort as a group that day and "zap" them by taking away their recess. It has to be clear to them that you did this for a reason, not just to prove that you can and will do it, so be sure that your reason for taking away a recess is a good one.

I believe that if you take away their recess on a warm, sunny Friday afternoon it is more effective, because they'll come to understand that they truly have to *earn* their recess each day. Think of this as an investment you're making for the rest of the year.

Please review pages 140-142, *carefully*, to get a better understanding of how I set this up and my thinking behind it. Feel free to call or e-mail me if you want to talk about this before trying it in your own classroom.

# DAY TWENTY-TWO

## Idea

*Make A McDeal*

The first couple weeks of school I put a lot of time and energy into getting the team up and running. By this time, I'm ready to really start focusing on individuals and their needs.

By now, in your classroom, I'll bet the majority of your students are buying into and working to make this one of their best years ever in school—especially if you've been consistently using this program and have been very consistent with your discipline. However, there may be one or two students who are still not buying into the program or are still testing your authority.

I usually have a couple of students each year who, for whatever reason, are not yet working with the team. I'll usually do one of the following things (or a combination of them) with these students to try and bring them into the fold:

**Strategy One:** I'll identify a couple of my strong leaders in the room to help work with me to encourage the struggling students to join the team. I believe that many times positive peer pressure can have a more powerful effect on students than I can.

For example, I may ask a student if they'd be willing to work with me to help another student who is struggling. This may include sitting next to them during class and helping them to stay on task. It may also include asking them to try to get that student involved with the group during recess and other less structured times during the day.

I tell this student that I chose them because they've shown leadership abilities on our team, and I need their help to make sure everyone feels a part of the team. I make it clear to them that this is not mandatory, but if they do take on this responsibility, I expect them to keep this private.

I'll offer to buy a McDonald's lunch for them, the student they're helping, and a buddy of their choice in a month's time, if they decide to help and do a good job.

> **NOTE:** My students will ask why I bought certain kids a McDonald's lunch. I tell them that throughout the year I'll be asking students to do special projects for me, and this is one way I offer to pay them back for their help. I also mention that sometimes I'll ask them to keep the special projects private, and we should all respect that.

**Strategy Two:** I'll identify a student who's struggling and tell them that I'm concerned that they're still not committed to our team goals. I'll ask them what I can do to help get them to commit.

I'll ask who in the room they'd most like to sit next to in class to help them stay focused. If I agree with their choice, I'll ask that student to sit next to them. I will again make it clear to the student this is **not mandatory**, but that I'll be willing to buy both students a McDonald's lunch, if all is going well after a month.

I may also put the student who's struggling on a contract where they can earn points each day based on behavior and completing their work on time. The points can be accumulated and turned in for specific rewards agreed upon by the student and myself.

**Strategy Three:** Identify the student in your room who seems to be struggling the most with the rules or with their classmates, and ask them to help you out with a special project. Tell them you need their help to manage the team. Explain that you need someone to be your helper to keep things running smoothly in the room, and that you'll buy them and a buddy a McDonald's lunch at the end of a month if they're doing a great job.

One year, I had a student who had been labeled as a class bully by former teachers. I noticed early on why he received this label. I tried this strategy with this kid, and was amazed by how he responded. He became one of my class leaders and was respected and liked by the entire class.

## DAY TWENTY-THREE

### Activity

*Success Stories — Part One*

1.  Review pages 212-214 to get an overview of this activity.

2.  Start collecting short stories about people who have overcome great setbacks in their lives or have accomplished something special by dreaming big, and then working to make it happen!

3.  Try to find one person a week to read about.

4.  Whenever possible, try to find a success story that will reinforce the "Success Skill of the Week" your class is focusing on in your room.

**NOTE:** There are many places to find short success stories to share with your students. Any of the *Chicken Soup for the Soul* books are an excellent place to look. You can also find inspirational stories in a magazine called *Bits and Pieces*, and a book by Cynthia Kersey, *Unstoppable*. Be sure to check the bibliography in the back of this book for more places to look.

**Idea:** You can even have the students make up success stories and turn them into a success story comic book to tie this into your writing curriculum. If you want to really challenge them, have them include all their spelling words from this week in their story.

# DAY TWENTY-FOUR

## Activity

### Partner Tag

Partner Tag is a game I learned while taking a theater class at Lansing Community College. This is a great team-building activity, which the class will want to play often. It's a game that's best played outdoors, because, your students will need plenty of room to move about the space. Follow these steps when setting up this activity:

1.  Have your students count off so that each person has a partner to begin the game. If you have 26 students, count 1 - 13 twice. (I'll explain what to do if you have an odd number of students in your class at the end of the steps to follow.)

2.  Explain that the object of the game is to never be IT, and the only way to become IT is to be tagged by the person who is IT.

3.  Partners must hold hands—one hand each. Let your students know they can never become IT as long as they're holding onto a partner's hand.

4.  Explain that once the game begins, everyone will be holding their partner's hand except for two people. One person will be IT, and the other person will be trying to find a new partner to hold hands with before being tagged by the person who is IT.

5.  The person without a partner, who is trying to find a person with whom to hold hands, can choose from any of the people who are already holding hands.

6.  Tell your students that if someone grabs the other hand of their partner, they must let go of their partner's hand and find a new partner, before being tagged IT, by grabbing the free hand of another person who has a partner.

7.    Share the following rules with your students to help clarify more details of how to play this game:

*Rules:*
   a.  You cannot have more than two people holding hands in each group.
   b.  If someone grabs your partner's other hand, you must let go of their hand and find a new partner.
   c.  Be sure to extend your hand to someone running towards you. You will automatically become IT if you refuse to let a person grab your hand.
   d.  If you let go of your partner's hand before someone else grabs their other hand, you automatically become IT.
   e.  If you are tagged, you may tag the person right back if they haven't found a hand to hold yet.

Once the game starts and everyone is running around, you may want to stop and tell the group that the only two people who need to run around are the person who is IT and the person looking to find someone's hand to hold onto.

Everyone else is safe as long as they're holding onto their partner's hand.

**NOTE:** If you have an odd number of students you can have one student sit out and take the place of the first student who lets go of their partner's hand too soon, or take the place of the student who refuses to hold a person's hand when they're approached. Both these situations just mentioned will occur many times throughout the game, so no one will sit out for very long.

# DAY TWENTY-FIVE

## Activity

*Coin Connection #2*

Hopefully, the coins are becoming an important symbol in your classroom to regularly help remind your students that they're working on their attendance, attitude and effort in order to have one of their best years ever in school—if not their best.

Here's another idea for how to use the coin in a fun way to help motivate your students to take good care of their coins and to make sure they have them every day.

Choose a homework assignment where you could offer the students a chance to do only half of it, *if* the person you randomly select (using your name sticks in a cup) can produce their coin and show it to the class.

Tell them you're willing to make this deal only if they promise you that they'll give the half assignment their very best effort.

Remind the class that throughout the year you'll continue to find different ways to reward them for having their coins, and that you'll make special little deals like this only during those times where you feel the team is working really well toward the team goals you set as a class.

**NOTE:** Speaking of homework assignments, I have an unwritten rule in my classroom that if I ever hear anyone complain or moan over a homework assignment, I'll double the assignment for the entire group. I've only had to double one or two assignments during the whole year. Because of this rule, I don't deal with daily headaches of kids groaning about having to do some work.

**Reminder:** Be sure to choose a new "Success Skill of the Week" to use with your students for the next two weeks if you haven't done so yet.

# DAY TWENTY-SIX

## Idea

*Help Wanted Letter For Parent Helpers*

Depending on what grade you teach, you may—or may not—have a lot of parents volunteering to come into your room to help out.

I've always taught 4th and 5th grade. I never asked for parent volunteers to help out in my room during the first seven or eight years of my career, because I never saw any of my peers doing it. I was also a little nervous at the thought of having a parent come in and "judge" my teaching.

I was lucky that a bold parent came to me and asked if they could come in and help out. Because of that very positive experience (review pages 197-198), I've asked for parent volunteers every year since.

At the beginning of each school year, I send home a "Help Wanted" note to parents, asking them whether they'd like to volunteer to help in my classroom and to tell me what they'd like to do when they come in.

Some parents like to run copies that I might need. Others will ask to work one-on-one with students or with small groups of students. Still others will ask whether they can help out with bulletin boards, displays and paperwork.

A few years ago, I had a parent become a mentor/tutor to one of my students. This girl's life story would break your heart. She'd been in and out of more foster homes in her short life than she could count. She struggled with a lot more than just academics in her life.

This parent came in religiously every Friday and worked with her for an hour or more, providing her with the one-to-one attention she needed so much. They actually became friends. This parent did more for this girl than I could ever dream of doing.

If you haven't asked for parent volunteers before, make it a goal to do so this year. Open house and during conferences are great times to ask for volunteers if you don't want to send a note home.

Finally, find a teacher who works at a lower grade level for some advice on this. Many of these teachers are masters at getting the most out of their parent volunteers and making it a powerful, positive experience for all involved.

# DAY TWENTY-SEVEN

## Activity

### Team Assist Awards

1. Review pages 203-204 for this activity.

2. Get in the habit of identifying a few students each month who've done something extraordinary for the team or have given extra effort to accomplish something special.

3. You can make a formal award presentation in front of the whole class, or you can put the award certificate on their desk before class so they see it when they come in to start their day.

   **BONUS IDEA:** Call each student's parent(s) when they receive the award to tell them how proud you are of their child's effort to help make the team stronger and how you appreciate them helping the team reach the goals set at the beginning of the year. This goes a long way in providing excellent customer service for your students and their parents.

# DAY TWENTY-EIGHT

## Activity

### *Changing Negatives Into Positives*

A few years back, my class developed this activity based on a game my wife and I started playing with our son, Joe, when he was six years old. I told my class the story about how whenever we caught someone in our family saying something negative we'd say, "Negative," while pointing our thumbs downward. Then we'd make that person reword their negative statement into a positive statement. Once the statement became positive, we'd say, "Positive," while pointing our thumbs up.

I know this sounds a bit kooky, but I once read somewhere that the way you word a question or statement will tell your brain what to focus on. For example, if someone says, "I can't do subtraction!" the brain will focus on the "can't." However, if the same person says, "I need to find a way to do subtraction!" the brain will focus on "find a way."

Anyway, when I told this little story to my class, they immediately picked up on it and started playing it with me. Every time I said something the least bit negative, they'd stick their thumb out facing downward and say, "Negative." I'd then reword my statement into a more positive comment.

Here's an example of how this game was played in my room. In the morning, I used to say, "*If* you earn recess today, we will go outside." They helped me change that to, "*When* you earn recess today, we will go outside."

I know that doesn't seem like much of a change, but they got so into this their hearing became very sensitive to anything that sounded the least bit negative. They felt when I said "if," I left a little room for doubt that they'd earn their recess.

This little activity forced all of us—in a very fun, positive way—to become more aware of how we worded things. Also, it left no room for "I can't" pity parties. Not only did they hold me to this standard, but they held each other to the same standard as well.

Again, I know this may sound too simple, but give it a try with your students. Once you start playing this, you'll be amazed at how many negative things are said during the course of a regular day. However, as time goes on, visitors to your room will be even more amazed at how positive your students sound!

# DAY TWENTY-NINE

## Activity

### One-On-One In One

1.    Review pages 195-196 for a recap of this activity.

2.    Find a student today who's been doing a really good job in your room and pull them out into the hallway for one minute to praise them.

3.    Try to repeat step two a few times over the next week to help turn this into a habit. Mark it down in your lesson plan book to remind you to do this if needed.

4.    During this same time, begin to target certain students you want to discipline, as well.

      Remember to try to stress the behavior or choice you're unhappy about, and be sure to end your conversation in a positive way. Remind them that you care about them and want to help them have their best year ever.

NOTE: Over the years, I've learned from experience that it's much better to wait to talk to a child UNTIL I'm confident I can do so in a calm manner. I have no problem letting my students know when I'm frustrated with them, but I try *not* to express that in an overly angry tone.

As the model to follow for my students, I try to speak as I would expect a police officer issuing me a ticket if I was pulled over for speeding. I believe they have every right to issue me the ticket if I'm speeding. However, they don't have a right to drag me out of my car and chastise me on the side of the road for all my neighbors to watch.

Discipline with dignity. Better yet, discipline *consistently* and with dignity!

**Reminder:** Speaking of discipline, don't forget to send home another "Behavior Report" at the end of the month—and every month from this point on.

# DAY THIRTY

## Activity

*Celebrate*

If you've consistently used this *Thirty Day Planner* for the past thirty days, you deserve to celebrate with your class, because you and your team are well on your way to having your *Best Year Ever!*

The following are three reasons why you should take some time today and celebrate with your team:

1.  You've made it through the hardest part of the year.

2.  The beginning of the year is like a rocket launch. It takes a lot of energy to get that rocket into orbit. I'm sure it's taken you a lot of time and energy to build your team and to create a caring community for it to thrive in. By now, you should be starting to see the results.

3.  *Best Year Ever!* is now a habit your team will use every day.

If it takes twenty-one days to make something a habit, then by now *Best Year Ever!* should be locked in. I can't imagine your students letting you stop doing all the positive things you've created with them during the last thirty days.

Try starting your day today without changing the "B.Y.E! Day Count" to 30 or greeting your students at the door when they come in, and saying, "Welcome, to day thirty of your *Best Year Ever!*" to start the day. Or better yet, go in today and ask the students for their coins back, and tell them you've decided to not focus on *Best Year Ever!* anymore.

My guess is that they won't let you stop using it now, even if you wanted to, which I know you don't!

It's important along this journey to stop every once in a while and celebrate your progress!

Take time today to survey your students about the first thirty days. Ask them what they liked most about the beginning of this year. Have them share their favorite activity related to *Best Year Ever!* Finally, be sure to ask them to raise their hands if they feel they're off to a good start in having one of their best years ever in school—if not their best.

Bring in some donuts and juice to celebrate this milestone. Make sure you explain to your students why you're having this celebration. Make sure you let them know you appreciate their hard work to get to this point and that this is only the beginning.

### Request: E-Mail Me

If you get a chance, please e-mail me, and let me know you've completed your first thirty days. I'd love to hear how things are going for you, and find out whether this planner helped establish a positive, safe and productive learning environment in your classroom.

# DAY THIRTY-ONE TO THE END OF YEAR

Now the real fun begins! You can continue to use the ideas and activities listed in this book as you continue to tackle the curriculum.

The more you get comfortable using *Best Year Ever!* in your daily routine, the more creative you'll become using it. The goal is not to feel you have to copy exactly what I've suggested or have done in my classroom but to strive to make this your own, so that it better matches your own teaching style.

I believe teaching—like theater, music and dance—is a performance art. As an artist, I've given you some basic tools to use as you begin to create your own masterpiece. Give yourself room to take risks, make mistakes and continue to try new things.

Like other performing artists, be sure you share your talents with others. The more you share your ideas and talk about your craft, the more you'll receive back.

Try to avoid the 'nay sayers' and negative people who are quick to shoot down your enthusiasm and love for what you're doing. Remember, misery loves company, so keep on your toes.

Find other educators who want to keep growing and perfecting their craft. Surround yourself with those teachers who still enjoy being surrounded by kids, and most of all, continue to find ways to make what you are doing fun!

**Make It Happen!**

# APPENDIX THREE

# QUOTES TO USE IN THE CLASSROOM

# QUOTES

This list of quotes can be used with your "Quote of the Day" activity each day in your classroom. I've arranged the quotes loosely into general categories. Don't feel you need to use them in any set order. However, you may want to put a mark by those you use, so you don't repeat them during the year.

## ATTENDANCE

These quotes have been placed under this heading because they express the importance of showing up, getting up after each fall, and having courage to try.

*The giant oak is an acorn that held its ground.*     Anonymous

*Here is the test to find whether your mission on earth is finished: If you're alive, it isn't.*     Richard Bach

*It ain't over 'til it's over.*     Yogi Berra

*Never give in. Never. Never. Never. Never.*     Winston Churchill

*Our greatest glory is not in never failing, but in rising every time we fail.*     Confucius

*A champion is the one who gets up . . . even when he can't.*     Jack Dempsey

*Many of life's failures are people who did not realize how close they were to success when they gave up.*     Thomas Edison

*Perseverance is not a long race; it is many short races, one after another.*     Walter Elliott

*Just don't give up trying to do what you really want to do. Where there's love and inspiration, I don't think you can go wrong.*
                                                        Ella Fitzgerald

*You can't build a reputation on what you're GOING to do.*
                                                        Henry Ford

*Every successful person finds that great success lies just beyond the point when they're convinced their ideas are not going to work.*
                                                        Napoleon Hill

*There is no failure except in no longer trying.*      Elbert Hubbard

*Fall seven times, stand up eight.*                    Japanese Proverb

*Don't watch the clock. Do what it does. Keep going.*  Sam Levenson

*In creating, the only hard thing is to begin.*  James Russell Lowell

*Lost time is never found again.*                      Thelonious Monk

*Trying times are not the times to stop trying.*       Ray Owen

*Let me tell you the secret that has led me to my goal. My strength lies solely in my tenacity.*                      Louis Pasteur

*The beginning is the most important part of the work.*       Plato

*Far better it is to dare mighty things, to win glorious triumphs even though checkered by failure, than to rank with those poor spirits who neither enjoy nor suffer much because they live in the gray twilight that knows neither victory nor defeat.*        Theodore Roosevelt

*Never let the fear of striking out get in your way.*    Babe Ruth

*It is not because things are difficult that we do not dare, it is because we do not dare that things are difficult.*    Seneca (Roman Philosopher)

*Our doubts are traitors, and make us lose the good we oft might win by fearing to attempt.*                  William Shakespeare

*You may have to fight a battle more than once to win it.*
                                                        Margaret Thatcher

*Nothing is so much to be feared as fear.*     Henry David Thoreau

*Procrastination is the fear of success.*          Denis Waitley

*The person who would like to make his dreams come true must stay awake.*                                Richard Wheeler

*I couldn't wait for success, so I went ahead without it.*
                                                Jonathan Winters

## ATTITUDE—PART ONE:
## Positive Outlook On Life

*Not to know is bad. Not to want to know is worse.*
                                                African Proverb

*You get what you expect.*                      Alvin Ailey

*He who has achieved success has lived well, laughed often, and loved much.*                              Bessie Anderson

*The most difficult thing in the world is to appreciate what we have—until we lose it.*                       Anonymous

*There are no great people; only great challenges that ordinary people are forced by circumstances to meet.*          Anonymous

*No one ever makes us mad. We grow angry as a result of our own choice.*                                     Anonymous

*Those who bring sunshine to the lives of others cannot keep it from themselves.*                           Sir James M. Barrie

*The secret of happiness is not in doing what one likes to do, but in liking what one has to do.*              Sir James M. Barrie

*Nothing is really work unless you would rather be doing something else.*                                        J.M. Barrie

*Worry does not empty tomorrow of its sorrow; it empties today of its strength.*        Corrie Ten Boom

*I finally figured out the only reason to be alive is to enjoy it.*        Rita Mae Brown

*Each laugh makes you ten years younger.*        Chinese Proverb

*The real secret of success is enthusiasm.*        Walter Chrysler

*Work is much more fun than fun.*        Noel Coward

*You can't sweep other people off their feet if you can't be swept off your own.*        Clarence Day

*Nothing great was ever achieved without enthusiasm.*        Ralph Waldo Emerson

*Happiness makes up in height for what it lacks in length.*        Robert Frost

*One doesn't discover new lands without consenting to lose sight of the shore for a very long time.*        André Gide

*Failure, rejection, and mistakes are the perfect stepping stones to success.*        Dr. Alan Goldberg

*Seven days without laughter makes one weak.*        Joel Goodman

*The greatest discovery of my generation is that a human being can alter his life by altering his attitude of mind.*        William James

*Opportunity knocks so many times that it has raw knuckles.*        Barry Neil Kaufman

*All that we need to make us happy is something to be enthusiastic about.*        Charles Kingsley

*There is no security on this earth, there is only opportunity.*        General Douglas MacArthur

*Nothing is interesting if you're not interested.*     Helen MacInness

*Find something you love to do  and you'll never have to work a day in your life.*                    Harvey Mackay

*No brain is stronger than its weakest think.*    Thomas L. Masson

*Winning the prize wasn't half as exciting as doing the work itself.*                    Maria Goeppert Mayer

*Life is what we make it. Always has been. Always will be.*                    Grandma Moses

*The way I see it, if you want the rainbow, you gotta put up with the rain.*                    Dolly Parton

*He who laughs, lasts.*                    Mary Pettibone Poole

*For as he thinketh in his heart, so is he.*                    Proverbs 23:7

*Passion persuades.*                    Anita Roddick

*Three words that will guarantee failure: could, should, won't.*                    Jim Rohn

*I am a kind of paranoiac in reverse. I suspect people plotting to make me happy.*                    J.D. Salinger

*Happiness is essentially a state of going somewhere wholeheartedly.*                    W.H. Sheldon

*There are two things to aim at in life: first, to get what you want; and after that to enjoy it. Only the wisest of people achieve the second.*                    Logan Pearsall Smith

*There is little difference in people, but that little difference makes a big difference. The little difference is attitude. The big difference is whether it is positive or negative.*                    W. Clement Stone

*Make sure that the career you choose is one you enjoy. If you don't enjoy what you're doing, it will be difficult to give the extra time, effort, and devotion it takes to be a success.*                    Kathy Whitworth

*Since life is short, we need to make it broad. Since life is brief, we need to make it bright.*          Ella Wheeler Wilcox

*When I look into the future, it's so bright, it burns my eyes.*
                                                    Oprah Winfrey

*It's what you learn after you know it all that counts.*
                                                    John Wooden

*Most people find fault like there's a reward for it.*          Zig Ziglar

## ATTITUDE—PART TWO:
## Believe You Can Achieve

*I am the greatest. I said that even before I knew I was. Don't tell me I can't do something. Don't tell me it's impossible. Don't tell me I'm not the greatest. I'm the double greatest.*

                                                    Muhammad Ali

*You can do anything you want to do in life, if you have a fierce belief in yourself, a strong will, a big heart, and some role models to inspire you.*          Tyrone "Muggsy" Bogues

*Success is a state of mind. If you want success, start seeing yourself as a success.*          Dr. Joyce Brothers

*The young do not know enough to be prudent, and therefore they attempt the impossible—and achieve it, generation after generation.*
                                                    Pearl S. Buck

*The block of granite, which is an obstacle on the path of the weak, becomes a stepping-stone on the path of the strong.*
                                                    Thomas Carlyle

*Success is the ability to go from one failure to another with no loss of enthusiasm.*          Winston Churchill

*To see a man beaten not by a better opponent, but by himself, is a*
*tragedy.*                                               Cus D'Amato

*I am looking for a lot of men who have an infinite capacity to not*
*know what can't be done.*                              Henry Ford

*The world is moving so fast these days that the man who says it*
*can't be done is generally interrupted by someone doing it.*
                                            Harry Emerson Fosdick

*If you want a quality, act as if you already had it. Try the "as if"*
*technique.*                                          William James

*I tried to block out all negative thoughts. I kept reading books on*
*faith that tell you to just keep exercising your faith and continue to*
*believe.*                                      Jackie Joyner-Kersee

*Optimism is the faith that leads to achievement.*     Helen Keller

*Be bold—and mighty forces will come to your aid.*      Basil King

*Enthusiasm = Knowledge + Belief + Commitment.*
                                               Wayne C. Lawrence

*Always bear in mind that your own resolution to success is more*
*important than any other one thing.*              Abraham Lincoln

*Success is a habit. Winning is a habit. Unfortunately, so is losing.*
                                                  Vince Lombardi

*The secret to success is to learn to accept the impossible, to do*
*without the indispensable, and bear the intolerable.*
                                                  Nelson Mandela

*Everything is possible for him who believes.*           Mark 9:23

*You gotta believe.*                                    Tug McGraw

*A wise man learns by the experience of others. An ordinary man*
*learns by his own experience. A fool learns by nobody's experience.*
                                                   Vern McLellan

*One chance is all you need.*                                    Jesse Owens

*Courage is doing what you're afraid to do.*    Eddie Rickenbacker

*Believe it or not.*                                        Robert Ripley

*The first principle of achievement is mental attitude. People begin to achieve when they begin to believe.*                              J.C. Roberts

*What we need is more people who specialize in the impossible.*
                                          Theodore Roethke

*If we want a thing badly enough, we can make it happen. If we let ourselves be discouraged, that is proof that our wanting was inadequate.*                              Dorothy Sayers

*The people who get on in this world are the people who get up and look for the circumstances they want, and, if they can't find them, make them.*                              George Bernard Shaw

*As long as you're going to think anyway — you might as well think BIG!*                                          Donald Trump

*Keep away from people who try to belittle your ambitions. Small people always do that, but the really great make you feel that you, too, can become great.*                              Mark Twain

*I have learned that success is to be measured not so much by the position that one has reached, as by the obstacles which he has overcome while trying to succeed.*              Booker T. Washington

*The thing always happens that you really believe in; and the belief in a thing makes it happen.*                          Frank Lloyd Wright

## EFFORT

*I hated every minute of the training, but I said, 'Don't quit. Suffer now and live the rest of your life as a champion.'*  Muhammad Ali

*If the power to do hard work is not talent, it is the best possible substitute for it.* Anonymous

*Half of getting what you want is knowing what you must give up to get it.* Dr. Robert Anthony

*You can have only two things in life, reasons or results. Reasons don't count.* Dr. Robert Anthony

*Bite off more than you can chew — then chew it.* Mary Kay Ash

*If I had to live my life over again, I'd make all the same mistakes — only sooner.* Tallulah Bankhead

*An alibi is a first cousin to excuse, and both make lousy relations.* Murray Chase

*If there is no struggle, there is no progress.* Frederick Douglass

*Efficiency is doing things right; effectiveness is doing right things.* Peter Drucker

*Results! Why, man, I have gotten a lot of results. I know several thousand things that won't work.* Thomas Edison

*Opportunity is missed by most people because it is dressed in overalls and looks like work.* Thomas Edison

*Genius is one percent inspiration and ninety-nine percent perspiration.* Thomas Edison

*The power of persistence, of enduring defeat and of gaining victory by defeats, is one of those forces which never loses its charm.* Ralph Waldo Emerson

*Never be satisfied with less than your very best effort. If you strive for the top and miss; you'll still beat the pack!* Gerald R. Ford

*Paying attention to simple little things that most people neglect make a few people rich.* Henry Ford

*To stand still is to fall behind.* Gordon Forward

*Quality is never an accident.*              Willa A. Foster

*The best way to escape a problem is to solve it.*    Brendan Francis

*A man will sometimes devote all his life to the development of one part of his body—the wishbone.*            Robert Frost

*First we form habits, then they form us. Conquer your bad habits, or they'll eventually conquer you.*         Dr. Rob Gilbert

*Always listen to experts. They'll tell you what can't be done and why. Then do it.*            Robert Heinlein

*If you add little to little, and do this often, soon that little will become great.*                Hesiod

*What is easy is seldom excellent.*        Samuel Johnson

*Obstacles don't have to stop you. If you run into a wall, don't turn around and give up. Figure out how to climb it, go through it, or work around it.*            Michael Jordan

*I am a great believer in luck, and I find the harder I work, the more I have of it.*            Stephen Leacock

*You can't stop the waves, but you can learn to surf.*            Dr. Jon Kabat-Zinn

*Experience is knowing a lot of things you shouldn't do.*            William S. Knudsen

*Small deeds done are better than great deeds planned.*            Peter Marshall

*If hard work is the key to success, most people would rather pick the lock.*           Claude McDonald

*Going slow doesn't prevent arriving.*    Nigerian Proverb

*Sports like baseball, football, basketball, and hockey develop muscles. That's why Americans have the strongest eyes in the world.*           Robert Orben

*The best preparation for tomorrow is to do today's work superbly well.*                                    Sir William Osler

*Proper preparation and practice prevent poor performance.*
                                             Robert W. Pike

*There is no sudden leap into the stratosphere. There is only advancing step by step, slowly and torturously, up the pyramid toward your goals.*                              Ben Stein

*Success is achieved only by those who try. When there is nothing to lose and everything to gain by trying—by all means try it!*
                                        W. Clement Stone

*Look at the day when you were supremely satisfied at its end. It's not a day when you lounge around doing nothing. It's when you've had everything to do and you've done it.*    Margaret Thatcher

*It is better to ask some of the questions than to know all the answers.*
                                           James Thurber

*Hard work is simply the accumulation of easy things I didn't do when I should have done them.*          Dr. Dale E. Turner

*Always do right; this will gratify some people and astonish the rest.*
                                             Mark Twain

*An activity becomes creative when the doer cares about doing it right, or better.*                            John Updike

*Don't play for safety—it's the most dangerous thing in the world.*
                                            Hugh Walpole

*Luck is opportunity meeting preparation.*         Maury Wills

*Doing the best at this moment puts you in the best place for the next moment.*                              Oprah Winfrey

*Do or do not. There is no try.*                           Yoda

*If you can walk, you can dance. If you can talk, you can sing.*
                                        Zimbabwean Proverb

*Quit now, you'll never make it. If you disregard this advice, you'll be halfway there.*                                        David Zucker

# IMAGINATION

*One of the nice things about problems is that a good many of them do not exist except in our imagination.*        Steve Allen

*I have no particular talent, I am merely extremely inquisitive.*
                                                Albert Einstein

*Imagination is more important than knowledge.*    Albert Einstein

*Your imagination is the preview to life's coming attractions.*
                                                Albert Einstein

*The ancestor of every action is a thought.*        Emerson

*Thinking is the hardest work there is, which is probably the reason why so few engage in it.*                        Henry Ford

*To know is nothing at all; to imagine is everything.*
                                                Anatole France

*Creativity can solve almost any problem.*        George Lois

*An idea is the most exciting thing there is.*        John Russell

*Discovery consists of looking at the same thing as everyone else and thinking something different.*        Albert Szent-György

# SETTING GOALS
# AND
# LIVING WITH PURPOSE

*Sketch out a map of possibilities; and then treat them as probabilities.*
                                                Bovee

*Wanting something is not enough. You must hunger for it.*
                                                        Les Brown

*Make no little plans; they have no magic to stir men's blood…Make big plans…aim high in hope and work.*        Daniel H. Burnham

*I would rather be a failure doing something I love than be a success doing something I hate.*        George Burns

*Believe in something larger than yourself.*        Barbara Bush

*If you want to be happy, set a goal that commands your thoughts, liberates your energy, and inspires your hopes.*  Andrew Carnegie

*The three grand essentials of happiness are: Something to do, someone to love, and something to hope for.*  Alexander Chalmers

*The best horse cannot wear two saddles.*        Chinese Proverb

*Anything less than a conscious commitment to the important is an unconscious commitment to the unimportant.*  Stephen R. Covey

*He who is fixed to a star does not change his mind.*
                                                        Leonardo da Vinci

*He not busy being born is busy dying.*        Bob Dylan

*If we all did the things we are capable of doing, we would literally astound ourselves.*        Thomas Edison

*It's never too late to be what you might have been.*        George Eliot

*All life is an experiment. The more experiments you make, the better.*
                                                        Ralph Waldo Emerson

*No life ever grows great until it is focused, dedicated, disciplined.*
                                                        Harry Emerson Fosdick

*Men, for the sake of getting a living, forget to live.*  Margaret Fuller

*Losers visualize the penalties of failure. Winners visualize the rewards of success.*        Dr. Rob Gilbert

*Strong lives are motivated by dynamic purposes.*
Kenneth Hildebrand

*The great thing in this world is not so much where we are, but in what direction we are moving.*      Oliver Wendell Holmes

*There is no defeat except from within, no really insurmountable barrier save our own inherent weakness of purpose.*      Elbert Hubbard

*Great minds have purposes, others have wishes.* Washington Irving

*Vision without action is a daydream. Action without vision is a nightmare.*      Japanese Proverb

*Our business in life is not to get ahead of others, but to get ahead of ourselves — to break our own records, to outstrip our yesterday by our today.*      Stewart B. Johnson

*A problem well stated is a problem half solved.*    Charles Kettering

*If you don't know where you are going, every road will get you nowhere.*      Henry Kissinger

*The biggest human temptation is to settle for too little.*
Thomas Merton

*Find a need and fill it.*      Ruth Stafford Peale

*Decide what you want out of life; look on the positive side; and never give up until you achieve it.*      Bill Porter

*You must do the thing you think you cannot do.* Eleanor Roosevelt

*In life there are no overachievers — only underachievers.*
Rich Ruffalo

*You have to know what you want to get it.*      Gertrude Stein

*I always wanted to be somebody, but I should have been more specific.*      Lily Tomlin

*Saddle your dreams afore you ride 'em.*      Mary Webb

# TEAMWORK

*The greatest ability is dependability.*                    Curt Berywall

*Acting is not a competition; everything must be done for the good of the film or else everybody loses.*                    Michael Caine

*You can make more friends in two months by becoming really interested in other people than you can in two years by trying to get other people interested in you.*                    Dale Carnegie

*I praise loudly; I blame softly.*                    Catherine II of Russia

*Treat your friends as you do your paintings—place them in the best light.*                    Jennie Jerome Churchill

*Team spirit is what gives so many companies an edge over their competitors.*                    George L. Clements

*You can't tell how much spirit a team has until it starts losing.*
                                                            Rocky Colavito

*No one is useless in the world who lightens the burden of another.*
                                                            Charles Dickens

*The greatest good you can do for others is not just to show your riches but to reveal to them their own.*                    Benjamin Disraeli

*When spider webs unite, they can tie up a lion.*   Ethiopian Proverb

*You can make it, but it's easier if you don't have to do it alone.*
                                                            Betty Ford

*Nobody can do everything, but everybody can do something, and if everybody does something, everything will get done.*
                                                            Gil Scott Heron

*It's time for us to turn to each other, not on each other.*
                                                            Jesse Jackson

*No one can whistle a symphony.*                    Halford E. Larcock

*People's minds are changed through observation and not through argument.*                                                    Will Rogers

*The most important single ingredient in the formula of success is the knack of getting along with people.*          Theodore Roosevelt

*A single twig breaks, but the bundle of twigs is strong.*  Tecumseh

*I use not all the brains I have, but all I can borrow.*
                                                    Woodrow Wilson

*You can't do it all yourself. Don't be afraid to rely on others to help you accomplish your goals.*                     Oprah Winfrey

# BIBLIOGRAPHY AND SUGGESTED READING LIST

# BIBLIOGRAPHY AND SUGGESTED READING LIST

*Bits & Pieces*, Mark Ragan, CEO and Publisher, Chicago, Illinois. Ragan's Motivational Resources, (a monthly magazine).

Blanchard, Kenneth, and Johnson, Spencer, *The One Minute Manager*: New York, Berkley Books, 1981.

Bristol, Claude M., and Shermon, Harold, *TNT The Power Within You*: New York, Simon and Schuster, 1954.

Canfield, Jack, and Hansen, Mark Victor, *Dare To Win:* New York, Berkley Books, 1994.

Douglas, Mack R., *Making A Habit Of Success*: New York, Galahad Books, 1999.

Hill, Napoleon, *Think And Grow Rich*: New York, Fawcett Crest, 1960.

Kagan, Spencer, *Cooperative Learning*: San Juan Capistrano, CA, Resources for Teachers, Inc., 1992.

Levering, Robert, and Moskowitz, Milton, *The 100 Best Companies To Work For In America*: New York, Plume, 1994.

Martin, Bill, Jr., and Archambault, John, *Knots on a Counting Rope*: New York, Henry Holt and Company, 1966.

Pitano, Rick, *Success Is A Choice*: New York, Broadway Books, 1997.

Schwartz, David J., *The Magic Of Thinking Big*: New York, Simon and Schuster, 1987.

Wong, Harry K., *First Days of School: How to Be an Effective Teacher:* Sunnyvale, CA, Wong, Harry K. Publications, 2004.

# BEST YEAR EVER! PRESS

Providing Positive Products to Help
Make It Happen!

For additional copies of *Best Year Ever!* (and coins), visit Bill Cecil's website:

www.BestYearEver.net
or
Call toll-free
800-690-1233
or Fax
630-682-8933

*Best Year Ever!* (ISBN-13: 978-0-9779411-8-6) is available through the publisher and your favorite book dealer. Call for quantity discounts.